Students Must Write

If you are to do well as a student, and progress in your chosen career, the ability to express yourself clearly, concisely and persuasively in writing is a skill you should be trying to develop.

Students Must Write is a guide to better writing for students of all subjects. It may be read either as an alternative to a course on written communication or to complement such a course.

This second edition provides straightforward advice on the essentials of scholarly writing, the choice and use of words, writing for easy reading, writing in tests and examinations, giving a short talk, writing letters and applications, and punctuation and spelling.

It includes more advice on answering questions in coursework; the use of numbers, tables and illustrations to support your writing; how to find information, cite sources and list bibliographic details correctly; how to prepare a dissertation, extended essay, term paper, or project report; and how to help yourself when using a word processor.

Robert Barrass is a Principal Lecturer at the University of Sunderland. His other books for students include *Study! A Guide to Effective Study Revision and Examination Techniques* (Chapman & Hall).

Students Must Write

A Guide to Better Writing in Coursework and Examinations

Second edition

Robert Barrass

London and New York

PE
1478
.B36
1995

First published 1982 by Methuen & Co Ltd

Reprinted 1983, 1984, 1987

Second edition published 1995
By Routledge
11 New Fetter Lane, London EC4P 4EE

Simultaneously published in the USA and Canada
by Routledge
29 West 35th Street, New York, NY 10001

© 1995 Robert Barrass

Typeset in Palatino by Datix International Limited, Bungay, Suffolk
Printed and bound in Great Britain by Clays Ltd, St. Ives PLC

British Library Cataloguing in Publication Data
A catalogue record for this book is available from the British Library

Library of Congress Cataloguing in Publication Data
A catalogue record for this book has been requested

ISBN 0–415–13222–3

Contents

Figures and tables

FIGURES

TABLES

Preface

The ability to express yourself clearly is an essential basis for success as a student, and when applying for employment, and in any career. In all academic subjects students must write, and all teachers and lecturers should encourage them to write well. This book, therefore, is for all students: for those who know that their written work does not give a true indication of their ability, and who are looking for help in putting their thoughts into words; for those who accept that if they could improve their writing they could score higher marks in all coursework and in examinations; and also for those who although satisfied that they write well are prepared to consider the possibility of improvement. By improving their writing all students should be able to improve the quality of their thinking – because writing and thinking are very closely associated – and by submitting better written work for assessment they should achieve higher grades.

In this second edition account is taken of many changes in higher education over the past twelve years. The order of presentation of some material has been changed to correspond more closely with students' needs – from the first to the final year of a degree course. I hope it will help all students, whether they entered university direct from school or college, are studying part time while in employment, or have returned to study full time after a period in employment. Changes have been made in all chapters and some have been completely revised, but the author's purpose has not changed. It is to provide a guide to better writing that students can read, perhaps one chapter each week when they start at university, and then keep on their bookshelves for reference throughout their studies.

In addition to the advice given in all chapters, suggestions at the end of most chapters – under the heading 'Improve your writing' – may be followed by students working alone or used by teachers as ideas for class exercises.

Robert Barrass
University of Sunderland

Acknowledgements

I write not as a grammarian but as a teacher, knowing how important it is that students should be able to think clearly and to express their thoughts effectively in writing.

For their help in preparing this second edition, I thank David Abel, Jonathan Barrass, Susan Cottam and Peter Harrison. I also thank my wife, Ann, for her help, and Adrian Burrows who drew the cartoons.

The comments of examiners included in Chapters 1 and 10 are based on their reports on examinations taken by eighteen-year-old students in the UK. I am grateful to the Secretaries of different examining boards who provided reports on A level examinations in all subjects. The memorandum by Winston Churchill (in Chapter 6) is Crown Copyright and is reproduced with the permission of the Controller of Her Majesty's Stationery Office. (Its PRO document reference is CAB 67/8.)

Chapter 1

Judged by your writing

If your long-term objective in study is to achieve your full potential, and obtain the highest grades of which you are capable, consider three reasons why many students underachieve:

1 Some lack motivation, and do not work hard enough.
2 Many attend classes and work hard, but have poor time management and other study skills.
3 More study effectively and know their work, but underachieve because they do not pay enough attention to improving their ability to communicate their thoughts in writing.

EFFECTIVE WRITING: THE BASIS FOR SUCCESS

As a student you use a pen more than any other instrument. You write for several hours each day in lectures, practical classes, seminars, tutorials, and private study. You score marks for all your written work, both indirectly if you make good notes and directly if you communicate your thoughts effectively. In assessed coursework you score marks for written reports and, as in examinations, for written answers to questions. So it is by your writing in coursework and examinations that assessors find out what you know and how much you understand, and judge the quality of your thinking.

Bear in mind, from the start of your course, that your final grades will depend not only on your knowledge and understanding of your subject but also on how well you write. In any subject, if two students are otherwise equal in ability and intelligence, the one who is the better able to convey thoughts effectively in writing will score the higher marks.

All education depends on the understanding and effective use of

Table 1 Judged by your writing

Characteristics of your writing?	Impression created
Writing clear	Considerate
Correct spelling	Well-educated
Punctuation and grammar good	Competent
Arguments well presented	Forceful, convincing, well organized
Writing illegible	Inconsiderate
Poor spelling	Lazy
Poor punctuation and grammar	Careless or uneducated
Arguments poorly presented	Incompetent

language. Writing is important in studying all subjects, and in all professions. Only by writing well can you give a good account of yourself as a student, and when applying for employment, and in a career when you write letters, instructions and reports. It is by your writing that others know you (see Table 1).

If you are to do well as a student, and progress in your chosen career, the ability to express yourself clearly, concisely and persuasively in writing is a skill you should be trying to develop.

The purpose of all education should be to teach students to think, and to write well so that they can express their thoughts effectively. Students should also be taught how to read critically – thinking about what they read – because reading, supported by personal observation and conversation, is the key to knowledge. There is nothing new in these suggestions. Dorothy L. Sayers, in *The Lost Tools of Learning* (London, Methuen, 1948), wrote:

> Modern education concentrates on teaching subjects, leaving the method of thinking, arguing and expressing one's conclusions to be picked up by the scholar as he goes along; . . . [Teachers] are doing for their pupils the work which the pupils themselves ought to do. For the sole true end of education is simply this: to teach men how to learn for themselves; and whatever instruction fails to do this is effort spent in vain.

Many students are clever enough to understand their work and yet unable to communicate their knowledge and ideas effectively. They need help with their writing more than further instruction in their chosen subjects.

Students are unlikely to appreciate that writing is so important in all subjects if the teacher of English is the only one who encourages them to improve their use of words. All teachers, therefore, should play their part in teaching the effective use of the English language.

Being so long in the lowest form I gained an immense advantage over the cleverer boys. . . . We were considered such dunces that we could learn only English. . . . I learned it thoroughly. Thus I got into my bones the essential structure of the ordinary English sentence — which is a noble thing. . . . Naturally I am biased in favour of boys learning English. I would make them all learn English: and then I would let the clever ones learn Latin as an honour, and Greek as a treat.

My Early Life, Winston Churchill
(1930; quoted by Partridge (see below), p. 3)

English . . . includes and transcends all subjects. It is for English people the whole means of expression, the attainment of which makes them articulate and intelligible human beings, able to inherit the past, to possess the present and to confront the future. It is English in this sense that we must teach our children all day long, at all stages in their school life . . .

English for the English, George Sampson
(1925; quoted by Partridge (see below), p. 3)

If only teachers [of all subjects] would teach their pupils to think out every problem, and insist that all questions be answered thoughtfully and clearly, this salutary and indeed indispensable discipline and exercise of the mind would immensely improve the pupils' speech and writing, not merely in the English class but also in every other, not merely in school but outside.

English: A Course for Human Beings, Eric Partridge
(London, Winchester, 1949, p. 112)

COULD YOU IMPROVE YOUR WRITING?

To emphasize the importance of writing in all subjects, and to help you consider the possibility of improving your own written work, here are some comments from examiners' reports on the writing of eighteen-year-old students.

English Language and Literature

Some students wrote with charm and intelligence, displaying a love of books and of scholarship. Their work, written in clear, direct and simple English, was a delight to read. Others with limited practice in essay, précis, summary and comprehension techniques were easily identified. And there were also candidates who displayed in their writing a contempt for our language.

Most candidates should spend more time thinking about the meaning of the question and the words used, and should plan their work. They would then be able to write a considered answer. With such thought, the standard of answers would be raised.

English Law

Many candidates took no notice of the actual question set. Instead they wrote *all that they knew* about the subject and thus not only wasted valuable time but also demonstrated that they did not have a proper understanding of the subject.

Too many candidates fail to appreciate that a lawyer cannot function without a command of accurate punctuation and grammar. Bad English means bad law.

Engineering Science

Particular attention is drawn to the deplorable English of some candidates . . . poor sentence construction . . . lack of lucidity . . . dreadful spelling. This is a pity because in both higher education and industry great importance is attached to comprehension and communication skills.

History

The best scripts revealed an excellent knowledge and understanding of the topic discussed; and an ability to write an organized, fluent and cogent answer.

Time spent on teaching the art of writing is not time wasted. Even weaker candidates obtain higher marks after they have been properly taught to plan their answers and then to write concisely, intelligibly and in an orderly manner.

Everyone is capable of self-improvement. Good candidates can do better. Inevitably, clever candidates do not do as well as they should if they have not been properly trained in examination techniques.

Geography

The best candidates showed skill and perception when interpreting questions and writing appropriate answers. But some students with a great fund of knowledge do not achieve their full potential because they are unable to make intelligent use of their material. If they are to score high marks, students must learn how to answer the different types of questions they encounter in examinations and they must acquire sound skills in composition and in basic examination techniques.

Unfortunately, there are many candidates who fail to benefit from their knowledge of geography because mistakes in grammar and spelling render them incapable of expressing themselves unambiguously.

Even the most able eighteen-year-olds, who sit scholarship examinations, do not write as well as they should. The following comments are from an examiner's report on a scholarship paper in biology.

All answers included much irrelevant information.
Looseness of expression indicated lack of careful thought.
Very few answers were comprehensive.
Even when they knew the answer many candidates had difficulty in bringing facts together in an effective order.
Many candidates had the knowledge but were unable to express themselves.

The best English is to be expected from students of English Literature but, in a paper on critical appreciation, the examiners note:

Standards of punctuation and spelling, as well as of grammar, are still declining. Even quite good candidates spell words as though they have never seen them before, varying their spelling from one occasion to the next. This decline in literacy, now *very* marked, should be a matter of great concern.

If clever school-leavers have difficulty with spelling, punctuation, and grammar, and in selecting, arranging, and expressing their thoughts, perhaps this indicates that there is something wrong with what is taught, and with how English is taught, in schools.

Students who are unable to express themselves clearly when they leave school do not suddenly acquire this ability when they enter higher education. They need encouragement, constructive criticism, and advice if they are to improve their basic writing skills. What is not perhaps so obvious is that even students who write well can, with encouragement and practice, improve their writing and so score higher marks in both assessed course work and examinations.

All teachers in schools and in higher education should help all their students to develop the ability to think − and to express thoughts clearly, convincingly, and persuasively − so that their writing is interesting and a pleasure to read.

IMPROVE YOUR WRITING

As a student you need to develop certain personal skills which, because they form the basis for success in any subject, are called core skills. Because they are needed for success in all subjects and all professions, these study skills are also called common skills, enterprise skills, or transferable skills (see Table 2).

Your style of writing reflects your whole personality, and developing your ability to express yourself clearly and convincingly in speaking and writing is part of your continuing personal development. So, before considering why students must write (Chapter 2) and how students should write (Chapter 3), consider three life skills needed to provide a firm foundation for effective study: self-management, money-management and time-management.

Self-management

Think of study as employment. Ask yourself why you are devoting several years of your life − full time or part time − to being a student. What would you like to achieve? To give direction to your work, you must recognize your long-term objectives. These may be: to progress on a particular course and achieve grades that are a true indication of your ability; to progress in a particular career. Consider how you are going to organize your life, as a student, to help you achieve your objectives:

Table 2 Some skills needed in any subject and any profession

Transferable skills	Why some students underachieve
1 Self-management	Personal problems
	Problems with relationships
2 Money management	Worries about money
3 Time management	Lack of planning: ineffective use of time
4 Summarizing	Not making good notes in organized classes and in private study
5 Finding information	Not making good use of libraries and other sources of ideas and information
6 Processing information	Not bringing together relevant information from lectures, seminars, tutorials, practical work, background reading, and other sources
7 Problem solving	Not thinking through issues to a satisfactory conclusion
8 Thinking and creativity	Mindless repetition of other people's thoughts: unwillingness to consider new approaches or different points of view
9 Communicating information and ideas	Not expressing thoughts clearly, concisely, and convincingly in speaking and writing

1 to ensure you have a balanced diet, with enough but not too much to eat and drink each day;
2 to ensure you take exercise, appropriate to your state of health, each day;
3 to ensure you have about eight hours' sleep each night, so that you are always alert when awake.

Money management

Financial planning is important, from the start of a full-time course, so that you can try to live within your means. If you work part time to increase your income, this will decrease the time available for private study and for other things that should be part of student life – and so may make it more difficult for you to achieve your long-term objectives.

Time management

As a student some of the time you devote to study is organized for you, as indicated in your timetable, but consider how you are going to use the rest of your time – each week – so that many hours are not lost in procrastination. For example, look at your timetable to see when there are periods during the day that you can use for working in the library – from the start of your course. Keep your long-term objectives in mind when you decide how many hours you will devote to study in the evenings and at weekends, and when you will take time off for recreation.

Set yourself medium-term objectives, by listing things you plan to achieve in each year of your course, in each semester, before your next vacation, and in each vacation.

Set yourself short-term objectives. Each week, consider what you have to do: establish an order of priorities, and then concentrate first on essentials.

Some students find they make most progress in a study session if they work not for three hours at one task but for one hour at each of three tasks, perhaps with a few minutes' break after each hour. But it is not possible to make rigid rules about such things – to suit everyone or every occasion.

At the end of your last study period, each day, list the things you plan to do on the next day, apart from attending organized classes. For example, you may need to read a chapter in your textbook, to consult a reference book in the library, or to ask your tutor a question. Number the tasks on your list to ensure you complete the most urgent first. If you do not complete some tasks on one day, reconsider your order of priorities when you prepare your list of things to be done on the next day. Organizing your studies, to promote effective learning and good work, and to avoid stress, is largely a matter of allocating your time and concentrating on essentials.

Chapter 2

Four reasons for writing

So much of what you write is intended for other people, enabling you to influence their thoughts and actions, that it is easy to overlook your other reasons for writing. You write as part of your day-to-day work: to help you to remember, to observe, and to think, as well as to communicate.

WRITING HELPS YOU TO REMEMBER

You probably first used writing as an aid to remembering in your early years at school when complete sentences were dictated by a teacher. Later, especially in the last two years, you made notes in class while a teacher was speaking, while you were reading, and during your own investigations.

Making good notes in lectures

At university you make more effective use of your time in each lecture, seminar or tutorial if you have made some preparations. You should therefore look at the syllabus or course guide so that you have an idea what is included in each part of the course; but remember that such documents are only guides. If you are expected to attend lectures and other organized classes it is essential to do so, to find out exactly what your course comprises.

Lecturers should provide, at the start of each part of the course: a list of subjects to be considered each week in lectures, seminars, or other organized classes; full bibliographic details of textbooks or other essential reading for this part of the course; and details of other learning resources recommended for private study. Without this information students cannot prepare for their next class, or view each class in the context of the course as a whole.

Students may also be provided with a list of learning outcomes (things they are expected to know, understand or be able to do by the end of the course). They should be told how their performance will be assessed, and should be able to purchase – or study in their own time – examination and test papers for at least the past two years of the course.

Each lecture should begin with a concise title, or a clear statement of the subject to be considered. You are advised to note the title, the lecturer's name, and the date. Then listen carefully, think, and try to understand. In speech more words are used than are necessary in writing, so you should not need to write all the time. Lecturers are likely to say something, and then rephrase what they have just said in an attempt to ensure that everyone understands. Then they may repeat things for emphasis; or summarize what they have said at the end of each part of their lecture to help you recognize and record the most important points. In taking notes, therefore, it is neither necessary, nor desirable, to record every word.

Take your cue from the lecturer. Sometimes, knowing that the information is not readily available from other sources, the lecturer may repeat important points for emphasis – almost as in a dictation. At other times the lecturer will speak quickly, and you will be able to write only carefully selected headings for each new subject discussed, and subheadings for each aspect of the subject (that is to say, for each topic).

Note the main points as key words and phrases. Use abbreviations. Record numbers, names, dates, and titles. Write definitions carefully as they are dictated. Record the lecturer's conclusions clearly and concisely.

Mark any points that you do not understand, perhaps by a question mark in the left-hand margin. Then you will be ready to ask questions at the end. Note the answers to your questions and listen to other questions and answers, noting anything that contributes to your understanding.

Copy simple diagrams carefully while the lecturer is drawing on a board. You should be allowed time to study any diagram or table projected on a screen or displayed as a map or chart, in silence, before the lecturer offers further explanation or moves on to the next topic.

Most lecturers write on a board or use transparencies on an overhead projector (a) to give their lecture a title; (b) to provide the main headings; (c) to emphasize certain aspects; and (d) to summarize essential points at the end. If the lecture has been well planned, your notes should contain a summary of the main points. These may be arranged as an orderly sequence of topic words and phrases, as numbered headings, with enough supporting detail (marked by letters: a, b, c, etc.) – similar to the outline prepared by the lecturer when deciding what to say.

However, keeping to the order in which a lecturer presents information – or develops ideas – is more important in some subjects than others. There is no one correct way to make notes. You may prefer to arrange them in some other way, which you find helps you to listen and to learn.

At first as a student you may take too many notes. With experience you are likely to become more selective, and as you develop your note-making skills you are likely to prepare different kinds of notes on different occasions – depending on the way a lecture or seminar is organized and on your purpose.

Remember that the lecturer's task is not to provide you with a neat set of notes – by dictating a summary of your textbook – but to provide a digest of the essentials of the subject supported by examples; to discuss problems, hypotheses and evidence; to explain difficult points, concepts and principles; to refer to sources of information; and to answer questions. In this way the lecturer acts as a pacemaker. By listening, thinking and understanding, you are able to move forward more quickly than would be possible if you worked alone. However, you will find it easier to understand and to make useful notes during a lecture if you have done some preliminary reading (see Table 3, p. 18) and if you have understood the earlier lectures in the same course.

You should either listen to the lecture and then go to your books, or make notes as you follow the lecturer's explanations, arguments, and conclusions. Whichever method you adopt, you should learn throughout the lecture and should be ready to ask or answer questions at the end.

Making notes helps you to remain attentive (see Figure 1) Selecting the most important points to record helps you to learn to distinguish what is most important from the supporting details. See also *Make notes as you read*, p. 109.

Good, concise notes help you to remember the essentials of a subject. They can be read and reread, and you can add to them throughout your course of study as you get a firmer grasp of your

Note-taking helps you remain attentive.

Figure 1 Make good notes so that you need not waste time rewriting them

subject. Good notes are an aid to all your studies and they are essential to revision before an examination, when you would not have time to read long and detailed notes.

Use wide-lined A4 paper (210 × 297 mm) for all your written work. Narrow-lined paper is not suitable either for your own notes or for coursework because there is no space between the lines for minor additions or corrections. In making notes leave wide margins on both sides of the sheet and leave gaps for additions. If you write on only one side of each page you will be able to insert extra pages of notes, in the most appropriate places, based on your observations in practical work, on your reading, and on your own thoughts. Your aim should be to have one set of notes that ties together all aspects of your work (see Figure 17, p. 111).

Making notes is an aid to concentration, to active study, and to learning. Because they are so important, try to make good notes from the start of any course. Some students use a bound notebook in which they make notes of many different lectures; but this does mean that when they go home they spend time copying them out. Most students use loose-leaf, wide-lined, A4 paper, and keep a separate folder for each subject. The use of loose-leaf paper has the following advantages.

1 Notes on any topic can be kept together.
2 Pages can be added or removed easily.
3 The order of topics can be changed.
4 Other relevant work can be kept in the same folder as your notes on the subject.
5 It is normally necessary to carry only notepaper and writing materials. Notes on each subject can then be transferred to the appropriate subject folder, kept at home, each evening.
6 This system also has the advantage that you are less likely to lose all your notes – the results of one, two, or three years' work.

Try to develop an effective note-taking technique so that you can make concise notes in all lectures, seminars, and tutorials. Then check your notes, as soon as possible after each class, while the ideas and information are fresh in your mind. Check that they are legible. Make corrections and minor additions. However, you are advised not to get into the habit of copying out your notes. This is likely to be a waste of time; and in copying you may make mistakes. Furthermore, if you attend several lectures each day, you will never have enough time to copy all your notes. Your study time is best spent on regular study, and on improving your notes as you learn more about your subject (see p. 111).

WRITING HELPS YOU TO OBSERVE

Preparing an accurate description, like making an accurate drawing, helps you to focus your attention on an object or event. When one point has been adequately covered in your description, look for something else to describe. This will help you to ensure that your description is complete (see Figure 2).

Observation is clearly more important in some subjects than in others but it is important in the arts as well as in the sciences and engineering. Description is the basis of journalism – the reporting of current events, and of history – the interpretation of records of past events. Similarly, observation is more important in some careers than in others.

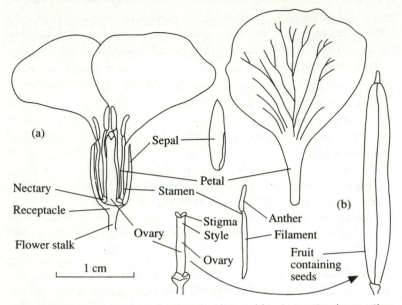

Figure 2 The preparation of a drawing is an aid to accurate observation, and an annotated drawing an aid to concise description: (a) the parts of a flower of *Cheiranthus cheiri*, the wallflower, and (b) the fruit that develops from the ovary

However, a carefully prepared description of an object or event may be part of any study. When appropriate, your writing – the whole or part of any composition – may be *descriptive* (a description of people, objects, scenes, etc.) or it may be *narrative* (a description of an event or sequence of events in chronological order).

The vividness of imaginative writing depends on accuracy and clarity, and its expressiveness on the choice and use of words; and in narration the right atmosphere has been created if the reader feels part of the scene, or as if witnessing the event described.

Making notes in practical work

As in a lecture, first write the date and then a title – whether your practical work is indoors or outside. Keep a record of what you do and of how you do it, of any materials or equipment used, and of any observations made.

If possible, your observations should be recorded on data sheets prepared in advance. Data sheets are tables in which the first column (the stub) may have the heading *Date* or *Time* and each of the other columns has a heading to indicate what was observed or measured each time entries were made, and the units of measurement (see p. 77). Preparing a data sheet, when the work is planned, helps you to decide what is to be recorded. During an investigation it reminds you when measurements have to be made, and helps you ensure that a complete record is kept. Then, after the investigation, because the data are neatly arranged, it facilitates your analysis of the data to derive results which may be included in your report of the work.

In practical work, notes should not be made in rough and copied out neatly later. As with lecture notes, this would be a waste of time (see Figure 1) and mistakes could be made in copying. Instead, legible and carefully worded sentences should be written when each observation is made, supplemented where appropriate by diagrams, annotated drawings (see Figure 2), or numbers recorded on data sheets.

Your practical notebook, like a diary, serves as a permanent record of what you did each day. But it is also the basis for any report of the whole work that you may need to prepare for other people.

WRITING HELPS YOU TO THINK

Capturing your thoughts

Students should get into the habit of making a note of useful thoughts that come to mind. Keep a few sheets of notepaper folded in your pocket so that you can note, for example, a topic outline for an essay, an idea for an interesting first paragraph or for an effective conclusion. Otherwise, your fleeting thoughts may be lost.

In *Goodbye to All That* (1957) Robert Graves describes a conversation with Thomas Hardy:

> He had once been pruning a tree when an idea for a story suddenly entered his head. The best story he had ever conceived, and it came complete with characters, setting, and even some of the dialogue. But not having pencil and paper with him, and wanting to finish his pruning before the weather broke, he took no notes. By the time he sat down at his table to recall the story, all was utterly gone. 'Always carry a pencil and paper', he said . . .

We may think in words or picture situations in our imagination; and then we use words to capture our thoughts and feelings for later consideration. Writing therefore is a creative process. Here are some quotations, from the works of famous people, that emphasize the connection between writing and thinking:

> Hardly any original thoughts on mental or social subjects ever make their way among mankind, or assume their proper importance in the minds even of their inventors, until aptly selected words or phrases have, as it were, nailed them down and held them fast.
>
> *A System of Logic*, John Stuart Mill (1875)

> The toil of writing and reconsideration may help to clear and fix many things that remain a little uncertain in my thoughts because they have never been fully stated, and I want to discover any lurking inconsistencies and unsuspected gaps. And I have a story.
>
> *The Passionate Friends*, H. G. Wells (1913)

> When someone says 'I'm no good at English', what he or she really means is . . . 'I'm no good at thinking straight, I can't talk sense, I'm no good at being myself'.
>
> *English for Pleasure*, L. A. G. Strong (London, Methuen, 1941)

> an English course consisting only of grammar would be very barren, and command of language is best obtained by using it as a vehicle for disciplining and recording thought and stimulating imaginative thinking.
>
> *The Language of Mathematics*, F. W. Land
> (London, John Murray, 1975, p. 258)

English is not like other school subjects: it is the condition of all academic life. The teaching of English is therefore the point at which all education must start.

Writing helps you to arrange your thoughts on any subject (see Table 3) and to plan your work (see Chapter 4). Preparing an essay or project report makes you set down what you know and helps you to recognize gaps in your knowledge. This leads you to a deeper understanding of your work and is a stimulus to further study.

WRITING HELPS YOU TO COMMUNICATE

As a result of the invention of the telephone in 1875 and of radio in

1901 we can speak to people who are not close enough for direct conversation. Before those inventions it was possible to communicate with such people only by writing. Nevertheless, though we can now converse with people who are in another place, and even see them on a screen at the same time, writing remains the more important means of communication.

If anything is agreed on the telephone, for example, it is always advisable to confirm in writing exactly what was agreed, so that both parties have a record of the conversation, and so that any misunderstandings can be corrected by further correspondence. Also, in preparing letters, reports, or any other written communications, there is more time for thought, for deciding what to say, and for deciding how best to say it, than would be possible in a telephone conversation. There is time to plan a composition, so that material is presented in a more effective order than would be possible in an unrehearsed conversation, and there is time to check and correct a first draft once it is complete, and if necessary to produce a revised and improved communication.

It is also worth remembering that speech, whether in direct conversation, by telephone, or over the radio, is still speech and is not in itself an innovation. People were speaking for many thousands of years before they developed writing and it is only by writing, especially since the invention of the printing press about five hundred years ago, that a great literature has been achieved and science has become a world-wide endeavour. The development of writing was a great innovation and it is still by writing that important communications are prepared — even if they are delivered as songs, plays, speeches, or talks.

IMPROVE YOUR WRITING

Listen and note

Your lecture notes help you to remember and are a basis for your further studies (see Table 3). They are not normally seen by the lecturer. However, at the start of a course, a lecturer may say at the beginning of a lecture that the notes you take will be collected at the end of the class. The lecture is then a test of the students' ability to understand what is said, to recognize and note important points, and to record enough supporting detail. After looking through the notes, the lecturer can help to clarify any misunderstandings and

Table 3 Making notes as an aid to thinking and learning

Before the lecture	In the lecture	After the lecture
Preliminary reading	Start on a new page	Check your notes
	Write date and title	Further
	Listen carefully	reading
	Make legible notes	Bibliographic details
	1 Headings ◄———————	Page numbers
	key words ◄———	Information and
	phrases ◄———	ideas
	2 Definitions	⎧ Observations in
	3 Conclusions	⎩ practical work
Prepare ◄—	4 References	Notes in practical
questions ——————►	Ask questions	notebook
	Listen to discussion	Think
	Make additions in	Learn
	gaps in your notes	Remember
	Understand	Store your notes in
	Learn	appropriate file

The preliminary reading will help you to understand the lecture better than would otherwise be possible, and to make better notes, as well as to prepare questions. The arrows in this table represent additions to your notes as a result of work done before and after the lecture.

advise those students who do not have a good record of the lecture as to how they can improve their note taking.

Observe and describe

A class of students may be asked to study and then describe a familiar object, or to observe and then describe an everyday event. Differences between the descriptions prepared by different students will result from differences in their ability to observe, to remember what they have observed, and to find appropriate words to express their observations. Differences may also be due to bias — to the observer's preconceived ideas which stand in the way of accurate reporting. This exercise provides a basis for a class discussion on the importance of writing as an aid to observation; and on the reasons for differences between descriptions of the same object or event.

Think and write

Keep a few sheets of notepaper in your pocket, and a pen, so that you can make a note of otherwise fleeting thoughts (as suggested on p. 15). Other suggestions on the use of writing as an aid to thinking are included at the end of Chapter 4.

Read good prose

To improve your ability to communicate in writing, read good prose regularly — for example, read books by established authors and leading articles in good newspapers.

Chapter 3

How students should write

In a novel or short story it is not necessary to explain everything. The writing is subjective — based on the author's imagination — and some things are left to the reader's imagination. In contrast, the written work of most students, most of the time, is objective: based on things we can observe with the five senses — which we think of as facts.

USE WORDS TO CONVEY YOUR THOUGHTS

Your purpose as a student, and in most professions, will be to communicate information and ideas clearly — with nothing left to the reader's imagination. To help you understand what is involved, consider a set of instructions as an example of a communication. We all use instructions: how to use a piece of equipment; how to make bread; how to write an essay. What do you expect when you use a set of instructions? That is to say, what are your needs as the reader or user?

1 *Explanation.* What are the instructions for? They must have an informative title or heading. What materials do you need to complete the task? In a recipe, immediately after the heading there is a list of ingredients. What do you have to do? The set of instructions is a clear explanation.
2 *Order.* You expect the task to be broken into separate steps, with each step distinct and the steps arranged in the right order — the order in which things have to be done — and preferably numbered so that you know you have completed one step before you proceed to the next.
3 *Clarity.* Each instruction should be a complete and carefully

'Tell them to send shorter messages'

Figure 3 Keep all communications short and to the point

constructed sentence so that the action required at each step cannot be misunderstood.

4 *Simplicity*. Only the information needed to help you complete the task should be provided. Any unnecessary words could be confusing.

5 *Completeness*. If an essential step were omitted you would be unable, by following the instructions, to complete the task.

6 *Accuracy*. You expect the writer to have worked through the instructions, while performing the task, to make sure there were no mistakes.

The need for sufficient explanation, the orderly presentation of your material, clarity, simplicity, completeness, and accuracy is most obvious in preparing instructions, but these things are essential in all except imaginative writing. Whatever you write, always prepare your work carefully.

1 Include sufficient explanation.

2 Arrange the parts of your composition in an effective order, according to your purpose.
3 Make your meaning clear throughout.
4 Convey your message as simply as you can (see Figure 3).
5 Make sure your work is complete: that nothing your readers need to know is omitted.
6 Check your work carefully and make any corrections, to try to ensure that every statement is accurate.

The writing of considerate authors, who by helping their readers also help themselves to convey information clearly and pleasurably, has all these and other characteristics which are now listed alphabetically, not in any order of importance:

accuracy (including no mistakes)
appropriateness (to the subject, to the reader, and to the occasion)
balance (showing an awareness of all sides of a question; maintaining a sense of proportion)
clarity
completeness
consistency (in the use of numbers, names, abbreviations, spelling, punctuation, etc.)
control (paying careful attention to arrangement, presentation and timing – so as to affect the reader in a chosen way)
explanation
impartiality (unbiased by preconceived ideas)
interest (holding the reader's attention)
objectivity (conclusions based on evidence, not on unsupported opinion)
order
persuasiveness (convincing the reader by evidence and argument)
precision (exact definition supported, as appropriate, by counting or by accurate measurement)
relevance (including no irrelevant material)
simplicity
sincerity (the quality of frankness, honesty)
unity (the quality of wholeness, coherence)

IMPROVE YOUR WRITING

Prepare a set of instructions

Preparing a set of instructions is a good test of your ability to communicate effectively. Prepare instructions on how to replace the batteries in a portable radio; or how to complete some other simple task. Then try to perform the task, following your own instructions. If necessary, revise your instructions. Then ask someone else to perform the task, to see if they can follow your instructions or suggest any improvements. You may find, if you look at a portable radio, that instructions on how to change the batteries are given by means of simple diagrams. Why is it desirable that such information should be conveyed without words?

A more interesting exercise, in which members of a class should first work alone, then in pairs, then as small committees, and then as a class with their tutor, is to write a set of instructions headed *How to write a set of instructions*. As a class exercise, this is perhaps best undertaken before considering the essential characteristics of scholarly writing (see pp. 21–2).

Read critically

The word criticize does not mean 'find fault with'. A theatre critic could report that a new play was excellent and say what was good about it, or at the other extreme advise – with reasons – why the play was not worth seeing. Most critics would write something about the plot, and about the acting, stating what they liked and commenting on aspects they considered could be improved, so that you could decide for yourself whether or not you were likely to enjoy the play.

Develop your own ability to think critically. Do not believe, without question, everything you see in print, or take it for granted that the author's is the only possible point of view. Does the author tell you what you need to know? Criticizing the work of others should help you to recognize good writing and to improve your own written work. Each of the following extracts, from a book or magazine, is followed by a note of some faults.

Extract from a geography textbook

Much of the Romagna of Italy, for instance, which was fully populated in ancient times, was only restored to its ancient population and productivity by great efforts in the present century.

Some faults

1 fully populated in ancient times	This is imprecise. How many? When?
2 only restored . . . by	This should read: restored . . . only by
3 to its ancient population	Very old people?
4 and productivity	As productive as in ancient times?

Extract from a book on examination technique

The complaints of examiners that students cannot write good English applies, I think, mainly to science students. Now science is founded on mathematics, and in general it is found that those who have an ability for literature are poor mathematicians and vice versa. . . . As their abilities lie outside literature, it is not surprising that science students write badly.

Some faults

1 The author should have written *either* that the complaints . . . apply, *or* that the complaint . . . applies.
2 The author is inconsistent: an opinion expressed in the first sentence is stated as a fact in the third.
3 The author makes the vague statement 'in general it is found that' but gives no evidence in support of this statement. In fact, some students of science write well and some students of literature write badly (see pp. 4 and 5). Many people are good at both arts and science subjects. No students need feel discouraged: the more effort they put into any subject the more they will understand and enjoy it.

Extract from a magazine article by a professor of education

The last ten years or so have seen changes in teaching of a magnitude unequalled in any previous period of our educational history. Such advances have necessitated a monumental expenditure of money and human resources, and it is interesting to note that whereas in countries like the United States . . .

Some faults

1 *Of a magnitude unequalled* means unequalled (see Table 16, p. 68).
2 *In any previous period of our educational history* means in our educational history (see Table 11, p. 56).

3 The *changes* mentioned in the first sentence are called *advances* in the second sentence.
4 *Advances* do not necessitate.
5 *Expenditure* cannot be monumental.
6 The words *it is interesting to note that* can be omitted without altering the meaning of the sentence (see Table 4, p. 33).
7 Are any countries like the United States? The author means in some countries, including the United States, . . .

Extract from a learned journal

Safe and efficient driving is a matter of living up to the psychological laws of locomotion in a spatial field. The driver's field of safe travel and his minimum stopping zone must accord with the objective possibilities; and a ratio greater than unity must be maintained between them. This is the basic principle. High speed, slippery road, night driving, sharp curves, heavy traffic and the like are dangerous, when they are, because they lower the field zone ratio.

Some faults
1 The writer's meaning is not clear. Does this mean that a driver should always be able to stop within the distance that can be seen to be clear?
2 The writer seems to have tried to make a simple subject unnecessarily complex.

Unclear, imprecise, and unnecessarily complex writing is to be found in the most unexpected places: in textbooks, in learned journals, and even in the work of literary critics:

Many people write obscurely 'because they have never taken the trouble to learn to write clearly'. This sort of obscurity you find too often . . . even in literary critics. Here it is indeed strange. You would have thought that men who passed their lives in the study of the great masters of literature would be sufficiently sensitive to the beauty of language to write, if not beautifully, at least with perspicuity. Yet you will find in their works sentence after sentence that you must read twice in order to discover the sense. Often you can only guess at it, for the writers have evidently not said what they intended.
Another cause of obscurity is that the writer is himself not

quite sure of his meaning. He has a vague impression of what he wants to say, but has not, either from lack of mental power or from laziness, exactly formulated it in his mind, and it is natural enough that he should not find a precise expression for a confused idea. This is due largely to the fact that many writers think, not before, but as they write.

The Summing Up, William Somerset Maugham (1938)

Practise writing

To be good at any sport, or to play any musical instrument well, you must practise regularly. Similarly, to write well you must practise writing: for example, by keeping a private diary in which you record your own experiences or by corresponding regularly with a friend. Then take trouble to convey your thoughts in carefully constructed unambiguous sentences, organized in paragraphs, and arranged in an appropriate order — so that you can understand your personal records, and so that your communications can be understood at first reading by the reader you have in mind.

You can also learn by considering the advice of experienced and successful authors:

Write as simply as you can — as though you were writing a letter to a friend.

William Somerset Maugham

Write as often as possible. Read good authors critically . . . noticing how they work.

J. B. Priestley

Never copy other writers. Never wait for inspiration. Get something down on paper . . . and look at it the next morning to see how you can improve it.

Nicholas Monserrat

Success depends upon natural talent developed by hard work.

Evelyn Waugh

If you write badly it is probably because you have not thought sufficiently about what you wish to say. To write well, write about things you know best and try to express your thoughts as clearly and simply as you can. Always think, before you begin, (a) whom you expect to interest; (b) what they need to know; and (c) how best to tell them.

Chapter 4

Answering questions in coursework

Except in note taking, when you write you are putting information and ideas together in your own way: you are composing. A letter to a friend; a written answer to a question in coursework or examinations; a memorandum to a colleague in business, management, production, or research; a report in a newspaper or a project report; an essay or an article in a magazine or journal: all these are compositions.

If you would like to improve your writing, you have taken the first step by recognizing the possibility of improvement. To ensure further improvement and so provide encouragement, prepare every composition, however small, in four stages. Always (a) think, (b) plan, (c) write, and (d) check your work.

The first two stages – thinking and planning – help you to make a start and take you well on the way to completing your work. In an examination only a few minutes can be devoted to thinking and planning, but in coursework much time may be spent on the search for information and ideas, and in discussion and thought. Irrespective of the time available, the first step must always be to decide what exactly is required.

THINK ABOUT THE QUESTION

In coursework your title will be the question you must answer. You should be given this in writing so that there is no possibility of misunderstandings. However, if the question is set in class do not take it down in note form or rely on another student to record it for you. To ensure accuracy, write every word and punctuation mark carefully yourself.

A good title will inform the reader, but before this it should enable you to define the purpose and scope of your composition. In preparing any communication the most important consideration is not what you know but what your readers need to know. In coursework and examinations each of your compositions will be marked by one reader who will require only an answer to the question set: no more, no less.

Analyse the question

The question set, your terms of reference, or your own title should concentrate your attention on the needs of your readers. The most common fault in students' written work, if they know their subject, is failure to answer precisely the question set, or the inclusion of irrelevant material. Some students read the question and immediately start to write all they know about the subject. It is as if they expected the marker to search for any relevant material, give credit for this even if it is not part of an organized answer to the question set, and ignore any irrelevant material. In fact, anything irrelevant — sometimes called padding — serves to obscure meaning. It makes clear to the reader only that the writer did not understand exactly what was required. By making relevant material harder to locate, any superfluous words or phrases actually make it harder for an assessor to award marks.

To make yourself think about exactly what is required, so that you include only relevant material, it is a good idea to start with a four-part analysis of the question. The word SARI will help you to remember the initial letters of four words.

Subject   What is the question about?

Aspect   You are never asked to write all you know about a subject. Which aspect or aspects of the subject must be covered in your answer to this question?

Restrictions Do any words limit the form or scope of your answer (for example, 'brief', 'concise', 'outline')?

Instructions Are any words instructions? If so, you must obey them (for example, compare, essay, explain, summarize). See also p. 60.

Analyse every question in this way, in both coursework and examinations. This need not take long and it will help you to ensure that in preparing your answer you respond to the exact wording of the question.

Stimulate your thoughts

Make notes as you analyse the question. Start with a blank sheet of A4 paper and record relevant thoughts as they come to mind. Spread key words, phrases, and sentences over a whole page, leaving plenty of space for additions. Use main points as headings (perhaps by selecting words from different parts of the question set) and note supporting details below relevant headings.

The person marking your work, like any other reader, wants relevant information and ideas well organized and clearly presented.

In a description your purpose is to produce in the mind of the reader a picture of the thing described. You should proceed from general characteristics to details, from the general to the particular (as with a definition – see p. 61), or perhaps from the outside to the inside (for example, of a building or piece of equipment).

In narration (see p. 14) the reader needs to know what happened, with some description, and would like to know how, and when, and where.

In exposition (explanation) the reader may need to know, for example, what it is, who may use it, and how it works.

Whatever you are writing, ask yourself the questions your reader would ask in conversation: What? Why? When? How? Where? Who? Add to your notes as you ask yourself these questions, which serve as mental tin-openers. Your answers will lead to further questions and allow you to make more notes.

Another way to stimulate your thoughts is to consider the different aspects of your course of study. Are any relevant to this composition? Be prepared to make use of relevant information and ideas from different sources. Different lecturers are concerned with different aspects of your course, but the information and ideas should be integrated in your mind, and in your revision notes, and where relevant used in your contributions to discussions and in your written answers to questions.

After a few minutes of thought and reflection, or longer if you have time, you will find you know much more about many topics than you at first supposed when you read the question set as an assignment or in an examination. If you were writing a letter to a friend or a report for an employer you would probably omit anything you expected the reader to know already. But in coursework or examinations, as a student, you must display your knowledge and understanding. You cannot omit definitions or important details because they seem obvious to you. Every question set is a test of what you know and of your ability to select what is relevant as part of an organized — well-structured — answer that makes clear your knowledge and the understanding that has resulted from your own thought after making use of appropriate sources of information. In short, each question is a test of your knowledge, of your ability to think critically, and of your ability to present your thoughts in an effective answer to this question.

PLAN YOUR ANSWER

The notes made as you are thinking are useful when you start to plan your answer. You may select some as topics for separate paragraphs and others as supporting points to be made in different paragraphs. You may leave out other points, in your selection of material, either because they provide unnecessary detail or because you choose better examples.

Select effective headings

Look again at the question and select appropriate headings to help you identify all parts of the question, to ensure you answer all parts of the question, and to ensure you answer them in an effective order — normally the order in which they appear in the question.

Headings are essential in your plan. They help you to think about your answer, to get things into an effective order, to avoid repetition, and to check that everything included is relevant not only to the question as a whole but also to the preceding heading. Good headings and subheadings are essential in most long compositions. They provide signposts for readers, but it is best not to use them in literary compositions (for example, essays in English literature), and some lecturers may advise you not to use them in any short composition. Also, what is encouraged in some subjects may be discouraged in others. Use them in your plan but not necessarily in your answer.

Prepare a plan: a topic outline

Making notes spread over a whole page, below relevant headings, enables you to record relevant thoughts. Then you can organize these, making them into a plan or topic outline, by numbering the headings as you make the following decisions.

1 How is the subject to be introduced? Normally there should be a short crisp introductory paragraph.
2 What is the topic for each of the other paragraphs?
3 What supporting information and ideas should be included in each paragraph?
4 Which of your notes should be deleted because, on second thoughts, you decide they are irrelevant, or provide unnecessary detail, or are not good examples?
5 What needs emphasis? Underline these points in your plan (but not in your composition – see p. 92).
6 Are any tables or diagrams needed? If so, where should they be placed in your composition? Knowing this, you can number them, include them in the most appropriate places in your answer, and refer to them in any part.
7 How can the paragraphs be best arranged – in an effective order?
8 What would be a suitable conclusion? Normally the last paragraph should be short and to the point.

These decisions about content and arrangement, made as you prepare your plan, provide a definite structure for your composition and make for easier reading: and so they help you to communicate information forcefully yet pleasurably to the reader. More than this, a well-structured composition displays both your knowledge and your understanding – your mastery of the subject – and helps you to convince an assessor and score good marks.

In an examination you may spend only five minutes thinking about a question and planning your answer, but as a result you will be able to write faster – once you start – and you will probably write more. You will produce a better-organized, more direct and more complete answer that the assessor will find easier to mark. In coursework you are advised to spend five or ten minutes thinking about a question, and making relevant notes, on the day it is set – perhaps on the same evening. Think again on the next day and spend fifteen minutes adding to your notes and making them into a topic outline. This may draw your attention to gaps in your knowledge and understanding: make a note of these. Thinking and planning in this way, before you look at your lecture notes, your textbook, or other sources of information, will serve to direct your attention to what is needed to answer each question and help you to give an answer (your answer) that is based on your own thoughts and is not just a rehash of things heard in lectures or read in a book. First consider what you know yourself. Think and plan, and only then refer to other sources of information – and if necessary revise your plan.

When you are happy with your plan, put it on one side for a while. This will enable you to have second thoughts, clarify your ideas, find additional information, and if necessary revise your plan. At this stage read the question again. Your topic outline should include all the points you consider necessary, in an appropriate order, as a basis for a balanced answer to the question set. Your aim should be to prepare a topic outline similar to the assessor's marking scheme – to be used in marking your work. It is easier to add new topics to your plan or to change the order of presentation of material at this stage than to change your mind once you have started to write.

MAINTAIN ORDER

Aristotle in *Poetics* said of a drama that it must have a beginning, a middle, and an end. So must a letter, an essay-type answer to a question set in coursework, a longer dissertation, or a report.

Each composition may be compared to an old-fashioned railway train, with an engine, a number of carriages, and a guard's van. In a composition such as an essay, the first paragraph (the introduction) and the last paragraph (the conclusion) serve different purposes, resulting from their positions at the beginning and the end (like the engine and the guard's van). Each of the other paragraphs (like the carriages of a train) is a distinct and essential part of the whole but it also links what has gone before with what is to follow.

After the title and the introductory paragraph, further paragraphs should be arranged so that they lead smoothly to the closing paragraph. An effective order may be, for example, the logical steps in an argument, a chronological sequence, or one geographical region after another. In a short work it may be an order of increasing importance, or in a long work an order of decreasing importance.

The first paragraph is your readers' first taste of what is to come. Here you must capture their interest. Your first paragraph must leave no doubt about the purpose and scope of the composition, but there are many ways of beginning (see p. 90).

Table 4 Introductory and connecting phrases that can usually be
          deleted without altering the meaning of the sentence

It is considered, in this connection, that . . .
From this point of view, it is relevant to mention that . . .
In regard to . . ., when we consider . . ., it is apparent that . . .
As far as . . . is concerned, it may be noted that . . .
It is of interest to note that . . . of course . . .
From this information it is clear that . . .
It has been established that, essentially, . . . in the case of . . .
In the field of . . . for your information . . . in actual fact . . .
    with reference to . . . in the last analysis

There should be one paragraph for each aspect of the subject (for
each topic) so that, as far as possible, you can deal completely with
each topic in one place. Like the composition as a whole, each
paragraph should have a beginning, a middle and an end: it should
therefore be well ordered and clearly relevant, with a limited and
well-defined purpose.

The topic for each paragraph is usually clearly stated (or is
apparent) in the first sentence; but in an explanation or argument
the topic sentence may come last. All sentences in the paragraph
should show your understanding of the topic. They may provide
relevant information or ideas, evidence, explanation, or an example,
and the first and last sentences should also help to link the
paragraphs so that the reader is led smoothly on from one paragraph
to the next.

Because the first and last words in a paragraph attract most
attention, never begin a paragraph with unimportant words. Omit
superfluous phrases such as *First let us consider . . . Secondly it must be
said that . . . An interesting example which should be mentioned in this
context is . . . Next it must be noted that . . . It goes without saying that
. . . We can sum up then by saying . . .* These thoughts should,
however, be going through your mind as you prepare your topic
outline. They are an aid to thinking and planning. How shall I
begin? What shall I say next? Then what? I can omit this. How shall
I conclude? Such thoughts help you but they are not for your
readers (who require only the results of your thinking); superfluous
introductory and connecting phrases (see Tables 4 and 5) merely
distract the reader's attention.

The change from one topic to the next should be signposted by a
clear break between the paragraphs. In a handwritten composition

Table 5 Introductory phrases that should usually be deleted

Introductory phrases	A possible interpretation
Arguably	I do not wish to commit myself
As is well known	I think
It is evident that	I think
It is perhaps true to say	I do not know what to think
It is generally agreed that	Some people think
All reasonable people think	I believe
For obvious reasons	I have no evidence
There is no doubt that	I am convinced
To be honest	I do not always tell the truth
As you know	This is superfluous
As mentioned earlier	This is superfluous
It is not necessary to stress the fact	I should not need to tell you
With respect	I think you are talking nonsense

the first word of each paragraph, apart from the introductory paragraph, should be indented. In a typed or word-processed composition, *either* the first word of each paragraph again should be indented, *or* one or two lines should be left blank between paragraphs.

After the paragraph break the reader is expecting a new topic, and the first sentence in most paragraphs is the topic sentence. The new topic is introduced directly and forcefully, usually in the first few words.

Within a paragraph, each sentence should convey one thought, or a few closely related thoughts. Punctuation marks should be used only when they are needed to clarify meaning or to make for easy reading (see Appendix 2). Each sentence should be obviously related to the preceding sentence and to the next. No new statement should be introduced abruptly and without warning. The sentences in each paragraph should therefore be in an effective order so that they hold together, develop a train of thought, and convey your meaning precisely.

Balance is important in writing, as in most things. The sentences in a paragraph and the paragraphs in an essay, like the handle and the blade of a knife, must be balanced in themselves and in relation to one another. Your composition as a whole must be well balanced: ideas of comparable importance must be given similar emphasis.

Paragraphing breaks up the page of writing, provides pauses at appropriate points in your composition, and helps the reader to know that it is time to pass from one topic to the next. Short paragraphs are the easiest to read and so they make for efficient communication. However, paragraphs are units of thought, each with one thought or with several closely connected thoughts, and they will therefore vary in length.

Only you can decide if your composition is so long that the reader needs a summary; but a short composition prepared in an examination or in coursework should not normally end with a summary. You should be able to make better use of your final paragraph: it is your last chance to affect the reader in a chosen way. The topics covered in your preceding paragraphs should have led to your conclusion; or they should have provided a basis for speculation; or they should allow you to emphasize some aspect of the subject which serves to link all paragraphs. Whatever method you adopt for bringing your composition to a close, the end should be obvious to the reader. It should not be necessary to begin the closing paragraph, as so many inexperienced writers do, with the words: 'In conclusion. . . .'

> Good paragraphs . . . vary in length, development, and organisation. They move . . . quickly through simple material and explain . . . any difficult points. Good paragraphs are carefully connected, and when there is a marked change in thought, there are enough indications to help readers follow the shift. Good paragraphs do not repeat unnecessarily or digress; instead they cover their subjects thoroughly and briefly. While their readers are still interested, the writing ends in a satisfactory final paragraph . . .
> *Effective Writing for Engineers, Managers, Scientists*, H. J. Tichy and S. Fourdrinier (New York and Chichester, Wiley, 2nd edn. 1988, p. 335)

WRITE YOUR ANSWER

Write in your own words

In any answer you prepare in coursework or examinations it is essential to show an awareness of relevant material explained in lectures or discussed in the seminars and tutorials that have formed part of your course. It is not usual to acknowledge these sources of information and ideas but it would obviously be a mistake to ignore things your lecturers consider important – especially if these lecturers will also assess your work.

Background reading will be recommended, to support your

lectures, seminars, tutorials, and practical work. From the start of your course, you must acknowledge the source of any published material used in your own compositions. To copy from a composition prepared by another student is cheating, and is obviously unacceptable. Similarly, to copy an extract from a book and present it as your own words is plagiarism – stealing someone else's thoughts – and is also unacceptable. Even if you summarize someone else's published thoughts, opinions, or findings, in your own words, you must still acknowledge their source. For advice on how to do this, see *Cite sources* (pp. 112–14) and *List references* (p. 114).

Background reading is important as a way of obtaining additional knowledge, a different approach, different interpretations of evidence, and new ideas. But it is not an alternative to thinking for yourself. You could not produce an original answer to the question set simply by copying relevant sentences from your lecture notes or from books. Also, each writer has a unique style of writing and if material is taken directly from different sources the changes in style will be obvious to the reader and will make for hard reading.

The time you spend on thinking and planning, before you start to write, enables you to exercise judgement in deciding what should be included and how it can best be presented. You make use of your own observations, and of information and ideas from different sources – which you must acknowledge – but having thought about the question to be answered, you must answer in your own way so that your answer will differ from those of other students in content, emphasis, and arrangement. You must convey your own thoughts – your knowledge and understanding – in your own words.

Use your topic outline as a guide

The time spent thinking and planning will help you to write a better answer than would otherwise have been possible. With your topic outline before you, as a guide, you can write with the whole composition in mind. Knowing how you will introduce the subject, the order of paragraphs, and how you will end, you can begin well, maintain order, make proper connections to help the reader follow your train of thought, avoid repetition by dealing with each topic fully in one paragraph, ensure relevance, emphasize your main points, write quickly, and arrive at an effective conclusion. In short, by working from your topic outline – your plan – you maintain control.

Write at one sitting

Your topic outline will be useful if you are unable to complete your composition at one sitting – because of its length, or an unforeseen interruption, or the pressure of other work. Many professional people write in a busy office or in places where they are constantly interrupted by enquiries from colleagues, by telephone conversations, and by other tasks. Similarly, as a student you get used to working in a library where there may be some distractions. Perhaps you read each day on a train to and from college, or work on a topic outline when you have a few moments between other tasks. However, if possible, when you have finished thinking and planning, and are ready to write, it is best to put other work on one side and to write where you will be free from interruptions or distractions.

With your topic outline complete, the theme chosen, and the end in sight, try to write your composition at one sitting. Use the words that first come to mind. Stopping for conversation, or to revise sentences already written, or to check the spelling of a word, or to search for a better word, may interrupt the flow of ideas and so destroy the spontaneity that gives freshness, interest, and unity to your writing. The time for revision is when the first draft is complete.

Work from your topic outline. Present information in a well ordered, interesting and straightforward way. Use enough words to make your meaning clear. Too few words will provide insufficient explanation and too many may obscure meaning and will waste the reader's time.

Arguments in favour of any idea expressed should be based on the evidence summarized in your composition. Where appropriate your statements should be supported by examples, so that the reader can judge their validity. Criticism of other people's work should be reasoned and not based on preconceived ideas for which you are able to present no evidence.

CHECK YOUR ANSWER

Two processes are involved in written communication. The first, in your mind, is the selection of words to express your thoughts. The second, in the mind of the reader, is the conversion of the written words into thoughts. The essential difficulty is in trying to ensure that the thoughts created in the mind of the reader are the same thoughts as were in your mind.

Too often, the reader is faced with an ambiguous sentence or a statement that is obviously incorrect and has to try to work out what the writer meant (see Table 5, p. 34). You will need to revise carefully to try to ensure that your words do record your thoughts. Try to ensure that the reader takes this same meaning.

A common failing in writing is to include things in one place which should be in another. Indeed, one of the most difficult tasks is to get everything into the most effective order. One reason for this, even after careful planning, is that we remember things as we write. Information and ideas may then be included in one paragraph although they would be better placed in another.

In writing we use words as they come to mind, but our first thoughts are not necessarily our best thoughts – and they may not be arranged in the most effective order. Wrong words and words out of place lead to ambiguity and distract the reader's attention, and so have less impact than would the right words in the right place. And inappropriate words, which are not suited to the reader or to the occasion, are barriers to easy communication.

By further thought, a writer should be able to improve a first draft. If possible, therefore, put your composition on one side for at least a day. Then be prepared to revise it carefully, if necessary, so that readers do not have to waste time on an uncorrected first draft which may reflect neither your intentions nor your ability. Read the whole composition aloud to ensure that it sounds well and that you have not written words or clumsy expressions that you would not use in speech.

To admit that you need to plan your work and that you can improve your first draft is not to say that you are unintelligent. The apparent spontaneity of easy-reading prose is the result of hard work (see Table 8, p. 45). Intelligence and effort are needed if a subject is to be presented as simply as possible. Simplicity in writing, as in a mathematical proof, is the outward sign of clarity of thought.

Every writer needs to correct and improve the first attempt. Flaubert (1821–80) had high self-imposed standards. He worked for hours at each page: writing, rewriting, reading aloud, and recasting, trying to achieve balance and perfection. Colette (1873–1954) wrote everything over and over again and would spend a whole morning working on one page. Maugham (1874–1965) said that if he achieved the effect of ease in his writing, it was only by strenuous effort. H. G. Wells (1866–1946) would write a first draft that was full of gaps, and then make changes between the lines and in the margin. Aldous Huxley (1894–1963) said, 'All my thoughts are second thoughts.'

Those who write best probably spend the most time criticizing and revising their prose, making it clear and concise but not stultified – and ensuring a smooth flow of ideas. However, revision must not be taken so far that the natural flow of words is lost. Alan Sillitoe said of *Saturday Night and Sunday Morning*: 'It had been turned down by several publishers but I had written it eight times, polished it, and could only spoil it by touching it again.'

In your work at school or college, you do not want to get into the habit of writing things more than once, and you will not be able to do so in examinations. Occasionally, however, you may rewrite an important essay or report, and even in examinations you should allow time to read through your answers – to make good any important omissions and to correct any obvious mistakes.

The pleasure to be derived from writing comes from the effort of creative activity – which should help you to learn about a subject and lead you to a deeper understanding. Each composition is original: it is a vehicle for self-expression, and involves you in organizing your thoughts and then presenting information and ideas *in your own way*. No one else would select the same material for inclusion, arrange the arguments in the same way, make the same criticisms or reach the same conclusions.

Pleasure comes from writing something that will affect other people. The reader may be persuaded or convinced by the evidence presented, or may be annoyed or misled by poor writing. Each communication is a challenge to you to present information and ideas directly and forcefully, to help the reader along, *and to affect the reader in a chosen way* – for this is the purpose of all exposition.

Assess your answer

For the person assessing your written work, the thoughts you express and the way your answer is organized are the only guides to the quality of your thinking. When the question is set you may be provided with information about how it will be assessed – explaining what is expected if a student is to achieve a particular grade. These assessment and grading criteria may apply to a particular question only, or they may be expressed in general terms (as in Table 7) so that they apply to any question that requires an essay-type answer.

You are likely to be told that presentation is important. A well-presented composition makes an immediate favourable impression on the reader. But consider what is involved in good presentation (see Table 6). Do not waste time on mere decoration, which can do nothing to make good deficiencies in other respects and which should have little or no influence on the mark awarded.

You are advised not to type or word-process coursework assignments, unless you are required to do so. In examinations it is not possible to use a typewriter or word processor, so in coursework it is best to get used to writing quickly on wide-lined A4 paper with a 2.5 cm ruled margin – similar to that provided in examinations. Legible handwriting is part of good presentation: and words or sentences that cannot be read obviously cannot score marks.

The world may be impressed by outward show but assessors in higher education and professional people in other employment should not be deceived by ornament. Neat writing or typing cannot make up, for example, for deficiencies in presentation resulting from: (a) an inability to use language confidently and correctly; (b) the use of inappropriate headings; or (c) the inclusion of information or ideas that are irrelevant or out of place.

Table 6 Ensuring your work is well presented

1   Start with your name, the date, and a title (see p. 121).
2   Use appropriate subheadings if these will help the reader (see pp. 30 and 91).
3   Leave a clear break between paragraphs (see pp. 33–4 and 121) and ensure an orderly arrangement of paragraphs (see p. 31) with no paragraph too long (see pp. 34–5).
4   Arrange sentences effectively in each paragraph (see p. 33).
5   Ensure each sentence is grammatically correct and unambiguous (see Appendix 2).
6   Use no more words than are needed to express your thoughts clearly and simply.
7   Use punctuation marks to help the reader understand each sentence at first reading (see Appendix 2).
8   Check the spelling of any word, if necessary, to make sure it is correct (see Appendix 3).
9   Number the pages.
10   Write legibly.

Table 7 Scoring marks for a written answer in a degree course

Standard of work	Mark out of ten	Grade
Outstanding *Presentation.* Work neat, well organized, and clearly expressed. *Length.* Appropriate. *Content.* Displaying knowledge and understanding of all aspects of a complete and correct answer to the question asked. Probably including information and ideas gained by reading beyond standard texts, knowledge of recent work, and, for the highest marks, original ideas.	8 +	A
Good Displaying knowledge of most or all aspects of a complete answer, but understanding not always made clear, and perhaps giving no indication of background reading. Perhaps longer than is necessary and including some irrelevant material.	6 +	B
Average *Answer incomplete:* does not include all essentials. Unnecessary repetition and *poor organization* may indicate an incomplete grasp of the subject, or an inability to communicate effectively. May include *irrelevant material,* indicating that the question was not properly understood.	5	C
Just acceptable	4	D
Answer inaccurate or incomplete. Not up to the required standard.	3	F
Displaying little knowledge and no understanding.	2	F
Displaying no knowledge or including only irrelevant material.	0	F

Source: Barrass, R. (1984) *Study! A Guide to Effective Study, Revision and Examination Techniques,* London and New York, Chapman & Hall.

IMPROVE YOUR WRITING

The word essay, from the French *essayer*, to try, is an attempt to cover a subject in a limited number of words. In an essay, as in any other composition, you attempt to interest the reader. You attempt to create a short original composition that is complete in itself. An essay has an accepted structure: a beginning (the introductory paragraph); a middle (a few paragraphs arranged in an appropriate sequence); and an end (the conclusion). Many other questions set for students, in both coursework and examinations, although they do not include the word essay, may require an answer with a similar structure: an introduction, an orderly sequence of paragraphs, and a conclusion.

Preparing written answers to questions helps you to recognize your strengths and provides an opportunity for you to make good any weaknesses. You will learn about the subject at each stage in composition: (a) as you think about the question and consider what could be included; (b) when gathering information and ideas; (c) from selecting and arranging your material as you prepare a topic outline; (d) from writing; and (e) as you check and if necessary revise your work. All the time spent on these different activities is time for thought. It is time well spent, because when your composition is complete your understanding of the subject will have been improved.

Always work to a topic outline when you write

If you have a choice of title, choose a subject that interests you, that you already know something about — or read about the subject before you start to write — so that you can select, arrange, and maintain control. As you think about the question, use one sheet of paper for rough work and reconsider these notes later when you make them into a topic outline. Organize your work, over the time allowed, so that you always have time for thinking and planning before you start to write.

Teachers of all subjects can help their students by asking for a topic outline to be handed in with each essay. Students should then learn from their teachers' corrections and suggestions, and should ask about anything that they do not understand or that they wish to discuss.

To give students practice in preparing and writing an essay in about thirty minutes (as they will have to do in an examination), teachers may as a class exercise set a question and ask for both a topic outline and an answer to be completed quickly.

Discuss your written work with other students

The power of rightly chosen words is great but there is no short cut to better writing. You can help yourself by noting the kinds of mistakes that most beginners make. Finding faults in the writing of others will help you to recognize your own mistakes and so to improve your own work.

Reading an essay to other students, as a small group in a tutorial, can provide a basis for discussion. Considering ideas on presentation, or topics for paragraphs, or points of detail may help all members of the group: they may learn more about their subject and about the art of composition. Consider the following common faults in students' written work.

Lack of planning. Information and ideas are presented in an ineffective order, or the orderly arrangement of the paragraphs is not apparent to the reader. Lack of planning is also indicated when information on one topic, which should be brought together in one paragraph, is included in different parts of the composition. This confuses the reader and makes marking more difficult.

Failure to answer the question. Some students answer the question that they would have liked, instead of the question asked. This results from lack of attention to the precise wording of the question, from lack of understanding, or from wishful thinking.

Lack of balance. Too much attention is paid to some aspects, too little to others, and some are even ignored. Such unbalanced or incomplete answers may be due to lack of planning rather than lack of knowledge.

Teachers and examiners, in order to be fair to all students, use a marking scheme in which a fixed number of marks is allocated to each aspect of an answer. In coursework and examinations you try to score marks. If you spend too much time on one aspect of an answer, you cannot score more than the number of marks allocated for this part. You are likely to get fewer marks for other aspects which you neglect. And you can score no marks for aspects which you ignore.

Failure to capture and hold the reader's interest. This fault also indicates a lack of planning. A student who wishes to interest the teacher must provide more than a summary of the teacher's own lecture. At least, you must select only relevant aspects of a lecture in answer to any question, and present them in an effective order. If possible, provide further evidence of your own thinking — by displaying knowledge gained from different lectures, from background reading or from personal observations, as appropriate. (See also Chapter 8.)

The use of a long word when a short word would serve the writer's purpose better and the use of more words than are needed to convey the intended meaning precisely. These faults may result from pomposity or from trying to make a little knowledge go a long way — perhaps in the belief that marks are given for the number of words used or the number of pages filled.

Lack of care. Many mistakes result from the student's failure to read through the composition. As a result, some sentences do not make sense, other sentences are ambiguous, and slips of the pen go uncorrected.

Criticizing compositions by other students will help you to improve your own. You will find it helpful, therefore, to look carefully at the written work of your friends — both before and after it has been marked. Similarly, you may benefit from their comments on your work. Can they understand every word and every sentence? Are they convinced by the evidence and by your arguments? Can they suggest improvements?

Prepare every composition in four stages

The basic advice given in this chapter, summarized in Table 8, applies to all writing, whether you use a pen or word processor.

Benefit from your assessors' criticisms

In coursework and examinations, you are usually trying to *explain* something *clearly* and *simply*. Remember that marks are given for *balance* (paying sufficient attention to each part of the question), for *accuracy* and *completeness*, and for the *orderly* presentation of *relevant* material: that is to say, for content and presentation.

When assessed coursework is returned to you, the mark awarded is of immediate interest as an indication of how close your work has come to the standard expected. But you also need to know what

Table 8 How to prepare a handwritten composition*

Think	1	Consider the title.
	2	Define the purpose and scope of your composition.
	3	Consider the time available and allocate your time to thinking, planning, writing . . .
	4	Decide who your readers are and what they need to know.
	5	Make notes of *relevant* information and ideas.
Plan	6	Prepare a topic outline.
	7	Underline the points that require most emphasis.
	8	Decide upon an effective beginning.
	9	Number the topics in an appropriate *order*.
	10	Decide upon an effective ending.
Write	11	Prepare handwritten compositions on wide-lined A4 paper with a 2.5 cm ruled margin – to leave yourself enough space for additions or corrections.
	12	See that you are free from interruption.
	13	Write your name and the title (usually the question set).
	14	Use your topic outline as a guide, so that you can keep to the point and keep going until your composition is complete – expressing your thoughts as *clearly* and *simply* as you can.
Revise	15	Leave yourself time to read through your work to check that every word is legible, that everything is relevant, and that nothing is repeated unintentionally; and to make any corrections or other minor improvements; and to check that all the points that you wished to emphasize are clearly made.
	16	If possible, put your composition on one side for a few days and then look at it afresh. Try to assess your own work, and revise it if necessary.
	17	Date all your work.

* For advice on word processing, see Appendix 1.

was good about your answer, whether it included any mistakes or misunderstandings, and whether the assessor has any suggestions that will help you to improve your written work. Consider every comment, correction or suggestion carefully to see how you can benefit from each assessor's advice. Such constructive criticism may be the only instruction in the art of writing you receive from most academics, and it is important because it applies directly to your own work – whereas a book for all students can give only general advice.

Learn from successful writers

Learn to improve your writing by studying the technique of successful essayists. Consider, for example, the purpose and scope of leading articles in good newspapers, and of articles in magazines.

Study each article carefully. Does the title of the article capture your interest? Does the opening sentence make you want to read the article?

Reconstruct the writer's topic outline by picking out the topic for each paragraph. Is each paragraph relevant to the title? Are the paragraphs in an appropriate order? Do they lead smoothly to an effective conclusion? Are the arguments convincing? Is the article biased? Are all your questions answered?

A tutor may photocopy an article, cut out the paragraphs, and photocopy them on separate sheets, so that it is not possible to see the order in which they were arranged. Then, as a class exercise, students can be asked to pick out the topic sentence in each paragraph, arrange the paragraphs in what they consider the most appropriate order, and then compare their arrangement with that of the original.

Chapter 5

Thoughts into words

Word games, such as Scrabble and crossword puzzles, are popular because there is fun to be had from words. Our pleasure and interest in words is not surprising, because when we speak or write we are trying to put our own thoughts into words. Indeed, the use of words is even more fundamental. Without words we cannot think; and we are limited in our ability to think by the number of words at our command. If we have a large vocabulary, and can construct effective sentences and paragraphs, we are better able to think and to express our feelings.

The habit of consulting a good dictionary (see p. 186) whenever you come across a word that you do not understand can be a lifelong source of enlightenment and pleasure. A dictionary provides excellent reading. As Eric Partridge (1949) pointed out in his *English: A Course for Human Beings* (London, Winchester), the stories in a dictionary are short but when you have read one you have learnt something:

> you understand the word the next time you see it in print or hear it spoken − and you can use it ... without your companions glancing at one another in that odd way which is so much more disconcerting than outright laughter.

We write so that we can tell others what we think, but if we use words incorrectly, or use words that our readers do not understand, we shall be misunderstood. We must think about words so that we can use them correctly and so that we can choose words that we expect our readers to know.

VOCABULARY

English is used for international communication, and people who read English as a second language are most likely to understand plain words in simply constructed sentences. If you wish to be widely understood, therefore, express your thoughts in simple language.

One of the delights of English is its rich vocabulary. No two words have quite the same meaning, and the choice of one word when some other word makes more sense will not help the reader. When *The Times* reported that Rudyard Kipling was to be paid £1 a word for an article, a student sent £1 and asked, 'Please send us one of your best words.' Kipling replied, 'Thanks.'

The right word is not always the first to come to mind, and people who have too few words at their command may fall back upon hackneyed phrases or clichés such as: *it goes without saying; at the psychological moment; in well-informed circles; feel compelled to admit; strange as it may seem; to all intents and purposes; with no shadow of doubt; in any shape or form*; and, *last but not least, conspicuous by his absence*. Instead, they should take trouble to find the word or words which express their meaning precisely.

> 'My dear, a rich vocabulary is the true hallmark of every intellectual person. Here now' − she burrowed into the mess on her bedside table and brought forth another pad and pencil − 'every time I say a word, or you hear a word, that you don't understand, write it down and I'll tell you what it means. Then you memorize it and soon you'll have a decent vocabulary. Oh, the adventure', she cried ecstatically, 'of moulding a little new life!' She made another sweeping gesture that somehow went wrong because she knocked over the coffee-pot and I immediately wrote down six new words which Auntie Mame said to scratch out and forget about.
>
> *Auntie Mame*, Patrick Dennis (1955)

You may use words that you understand, and that your readers understand, yet still write sentences that are difficult to read. In learning your own language you were probably encouraged to develop your ability to use long words, write complex sentences, exercise your imagination, and include adjectives, metaphors, and similes to make your descriptions more vivid or colourful.

But in most scholarly writing your purpose will be to convey your meaning as clearly and simply as you can. Long involved sentences, with many long words, make for hard reading. So, never use long words simply for effect. Prefer a short word to a long one (see Table 9) unless the long word is more suitable; and prefer a single word to a phrase (see Table 16) if brevity makes for clarity.

In *David Copperfield*, by Charles Dickens (1850), Mr Micawber had the habit of using long words to impress and then providing a translation so that he could be understood:

> 'Under the impression', said Mr Micawber, 'that your peregrinations in this metropolis have not as yet been extensive, and that you might have some difficulty in penetrating the arcana of the Modern Babylon in the direction of the City Road – in short,' said Mr Micawber, in another burst of confidence, 'that you might lose yourself . . .'

Some people like fashionable words, such as chairperson, currently, deprived, dialogue, escalation, hopefully, importantly, informed, integrated, interface, meaningful, nice, non-event, obscene, ongoing, overall, paradigm, relevant, situation, supportive, syndrome, traumatic, within, and workshop. The rapid dating of such fashionable words is particularly clear in euphemisms for *poor* people. They became *needy*, then *deprived*, then *disadvantaged*, and then *underprivileged* – yet remained poor.

Fashionable words may lose their impact through overuse. They may be devalued if they are used even when another word would be more appropriate. Discerning writers may then avoid such words, with the result that they may be words to avoid even after they have gone out of fashion.

When people think something is too technical for them, it may be that the writing is at fault. Unfortunately, some writers seem to think scholarly writing must be hard reading, and that they impress people by adopting a pompous style. But their studied avoidance of short words is not likely to impress, and is very likely to annoy, confuse, or amuse. This anonymous nursery rhyme pokes fun at grandiloquence.

> Scintillate, scintillate, globule aurific,
> Fain would I fathom thy nature specific,
> Loftily poised in the ether capacious,
> Strongly resembling a gem carbonaceous.

You know the rhyme? Perhaps you have heard something like it.

Table 9 Prefer a short word to a long word if the short word is more appropriate

Prefer this . . .	to this
yes	absolutely
do	accomplish
enough	adequate
extra	additional
expect	anticipate
use	application
about	approximately
help	assistance
begin	commence
about	concerning
so	consequently
much	considerable
now	currently
show	demonstrate
give	donate
meet	encounter
except	excepting
build	fabricate
first	firstly
send	forward
guidance	guidelines
people	humans
suggest	hypothesize
important	importantly
sign	indication
person	individual
people	individuals
please	kindly
methods	methodology
change	modification
partly	partially
people	persons or personnel
nearly	practically
soon	presently
preventive	preventative
go	proceed
about	regarding
is	represents
show	reveal
simple	simplistic
shortened	streamlined
later	subsequently
enough	sufficient
end	terminate

Prefer this . . .	to this
happen	transpire
use	utilize or utilization
almost	virtually
in	within

THE MEANING OF WORDS

As a guide to the meaning of words, to their origins, and to spelling, there should be a good dictionary on your bookshelf (see p. 186).

The habit of writing a word in quotation marks (in quotes: inverted commas) to indicate that it is not quite the right word, or that you are not using it in the usual sense, or that more is implied than is said, is likely to confuse people. Instead, always choose the word or words which convey your meaning precisely.

Many people confuse the following: accept (receive) with except (not including); advice (counsel) with advise (to give advice); advise with inform (to tell); amount (for mass or volume) with number (of things counted); affect (to influence) with effect (to cause *or* a result); complement (to make complete) with compliment (to congratulate); defective (not working properly) with deficient (without some essential); dependant (one who is dependent) with dependent (relying upon); deprecate (disapprove) with depreciate (decrease in value); enquiry (a question) with inquiry (an investigation); farther (more distant) with further (additional); fewer (in number) with less (in quantity); forego (go before) with forgo (go without); fortunate (lucky or prosperous) with fortuitous (accidental); its (possessive) with it's (it is); a licence (a permit) with to license (to grant a permit); majority (the greater number or part) with most (nearly all); of course (certainly) with off course (not on course); each other (which refers to two) with one another (referring to more than two); practical (not theoretical) with practicable (feasible); a practice (a noun) with to practise (a verb); principle (a truth) with principal (main); stationary (not moving) with stationery (writing paper); to (as in to go) with too (as in too much); true (real) with valid (sound); uninterested (not interested) with disinterested (impartial); venal (person who may be bought) with venial (pardonable); verbal (using words) with oral (spoken).

Approximate(ly) means very close(ly) and should not be used when *about* or *roughly* would do better.

Data (L. *dare*, to give) refers to things given or observations (facts of any kind) and should not be confused with *results* (which are obtained by the analysis of data).

Infer does not mean the same as *imply*. The writer or speaker implies something but the reader or listener infers.

Initiate means begin something; to *instigate* is to persuade someone else to do something.

Integral. An integer is a whole number or a thing complete in itself. Do not write integral part (meaning a whole part, not a part of a part) if you mean simply a part.

Often: 'People who eat mushrooms often die.' (But people who do not eat them die only once?) 'I often eat fish on Friday' (whereas most people, if they eat fish on Friday, do so only once). Do not write *often* if you mean *many* or *most*.

Parameters (Greek *para* about, *metron* measure) are estimators of population statistics based on samples. For instance, the sample mean is an estimator of the population mean, which it is not usually possible or practicable to measure. Prefer the word *boundary* or *limit* if one of these words conveys your meaning.

Refute should be used in the sense of proving falsity or error. It is not a synonym for deny or repudiate.

Since is a word that can confuse readers, or stand in the way of understanding at first reading, if used to mean as or because. It is best to use since only to mean a period of time.

While means at the same time as: 'Nero fiddled while Rome burned.' Do not write while if you mean *and* or *but*: 'I prefer squash while you prefer tennis'; 'On Saturday I work while on Sunday I rest'.

Within conveys the idea of enclosing: within the walls, within the law, within stated limits. It is an over-used word that for most purposes we could do without. Do not write within if you mean simply in.

Write *consists of* or *comprise* (not comprise of); write *different from* (not different to); and write *superior to* (not superior than).

Certain other words and the prepositions that should follow them, according to accepted usage, are the following: absolve from, abstain from, accompanied by, in accordance with, amenable to, collaborate with, compatible with, confirm in, conform to, connive at, consequent upon, correspond to (a thing), correspond with (a person), concur in (an opinion), concur with (a person), defer to, deficient in, impervious to, indifferent to, indicative of, independent of, irrespective of, ineligible for, militate against, oblivious of, preferable to, preoccupied with, refrain from, responsible for (an action), responsible to (a person), substitute for, but replace by.

Many people misuse the following words: access (for excess); aggravate (for annoy); alibi (for excuse); allude (for refer); alternatively (for alternately); alternative (for choice); always (for everywhere); appreciate (for understand); biannual (for biennial); centre (for middle); centred around (for centred on); circle (for disc); continual (for continuous); degree (for extent); discreet (for discrete); either (for each or both); elicit (for illicit); especially (for specially); except (for unless); feel (for think); generally (for usually); if (for although); improvement (for alteration or change); inform (for influence); lengthy (for long); limited (for few, small, slight or narrow); major (for great); majority (for most); the vast majority (for nearly all); may be (for maybe); minor (for little); natural (for normal); notable (for noticeable); optimistic (for hopeful); optimum (for highest); percentage (for some); practically (for almost); provided that (for if); quite (for entirely or rather); same (for identical); several (for some); singular or unique (for notable or rare); often (for in many places); some times (for sometimes); sometimes (referring to place instead of time); superior (for better than); to (for too); transpire (for happen); view (for opinion); virtually (for almost); volume (for amount); weather (for climate); wastage (for waste); and while (for although, but, or and). Consult a dictionary if you are uncertain of the meaning of any of these words.

Words may take on new meanings when people need to convey new ideas (or new words may be invented). The word broadcast used to mean the spreading of grains, but it is now used to mean the spreading of words – first by wireless (old word) and then by radio (a new word).

The meaning of words may change so much that they lose their value. They no longer convey meaning precisely. The new use may remain incorrect or it may gradually gain acceptance. Consider the following words.

A *democracy* is a state practising government by the people, but this word has been abused by countries in which the citizens have no political rights.

Literally is a word that should be used rarely, if at all, by most writers. It means actually, and is usually superfluous or otherwise incorrect (see Table 10). Literally means without exaggeration, yet it is commonly used in an attempt to affirm the truth of an exaggeration. For example: 'My eyes were literally glued to the television screen.'

Progress means a move forward, an improvement, a change from worse to better, but the word is misused for change of any kind. Indeed, the most outrageous suggestion may seem to acquire a certain respectability if someone calls it an improvement or progress. Consider, however, the monologue by Herbert Mundin (1926) about London's last cabby (cabman):

> It does not always happen
> That a change is for the good.
> More often it's the opposite
> I find.

Sophisticated was an uncomplimentary word, implying sophistry or artfulness, but it is now commonly used to mean complicated or to imply that a new instrument is in some way better than an earlier model. It is, in this context, an imprecise word that conveys no information.

Viable is a term that denotes the capacity to live, but in other contexts *not viable* may mean not competitive or will not work.

Vital means essential to life and this word should not be used in other contexts.

Words with only one meaning should not be qualified (see Table 10). *Facts*, for example, are verified past events – things known to be true. It is wrong, therefore, to refer to the *fact* that energy *may* be involved, or to write that the *evidence* points to the *fact* or that someone has got his *facts wrong*, and to speak of the *actual facts* is to say the same thing twice (see Table 11). Similarly, *unique* means the only one of its kind. Do not write *quite unique*: this is an unnecessary qualification of the word (see Table 10). And perhaps those who write *almost unique* mean rare.

THE WORDS OF YOUR SUBJECT

Easy communication between specialists depends upon their use of the special terms of their art, craft, or science: these are called technical terms. However, such terms may also be a barrier to communication (see Figure 4). Students should show their understand-

Table 10 The incorrect qualification of words

Incorrect	Correct
absolutely perfect	perfect
in actual fact	in fact
they are in fact	they are
the actual number	the number
not actually true	untrue
a categorical denial	a denial
completely surrounded	surrounded
conclusive proof	proof
definitely correct	correct
deliberately avoided	avoided
an essential condition	a condition
facing up to	facing
they genuinely attempted	they attempted
genuinely sorry	sorry
hard evidence	evidence
limited in amount	small
streamlined in appearance	streamlined
hilly in character	hilly
blue in colour	blue
few in number	few
seasonal in occurrence	seasonal
stunted in growth	stunted
conical in shape	conical
small in size	small
literally impermeable	impermeable
positively rejected	rejected
quite correct	correct
quite unique	unique
a real pleasure	a pleasure
realistic justification	justification
they really are	they are
really dangerous	dangerous
really impossible	impossible
very real problems	problems
refer back	refer, or refer again
the smallest possible minimum	the minimum
very necessary	necessary
very relevant	relevant
very true	true
wholly new	new

ing of the technical terms of their subject by using them correctly in appropriate contexts or, when necessary, by a precise and complete definition.

Table 11 Tautology: saying the same thing twice using different words

Tautology	Meaning
postponed to a later date	postponed
related to each other	related
still in use today	still in use
link together	link
percolate down	percolate
a tentative hypothesis	a hypothesis
ask the question whether	ask whether
on Friday 25 December next	on 25 December
the reason for this is because	because
in actual fact	in fact
one after another in succession	in succession
in the rural countryside	in the countryside
as an extra added bonus	as a bonus
my own personal opinion	my opinion
I tentatively suggest	I suggest
by advance planning	by planning
will disappear from sight	will disappear
in two equal halves	in halves
continue to remain	remain
symptoms indicative of	symptoms
a temporary loan	a loan
but . . . however	but *or* however
enclosed with this letter	enclosed
or alternatively	alternatively
equally as good	equally good *or* as good
an assassination attempt on the life of	an attempt on the life of
reverted back to woodland again	reverted to woodland
in the field of agriculture	in agriculture
each individual person	each person
every individual one	every one
may possibly go	may go
superimposed over each other	superimposed
grouped together	grouped
on pages 1–4 inclusive	on pages 1–4
from now on through until the end of December	until the end of December

Specialists who hope to interest non-specialists should not use technical terms without explanation. And authors of textbooks should not introduce new words without defining them: they should appreciate that learning an additional vocabulary may be a considerable burden for anyone coming new to a subject, and should therefore present their subject as simply as they can.

Well . . . er . . . this is it.

Figure 4 Use words you expect your readers to understand

When you write a technical term, you make two assumptions that are not always justified. You assume that the reader (a) is familiar with the concept, and (b) recognizes the concept by its technical name. Before using a technical term, therefore, you should consider whether or not it will help your readers. Technical terms should not be used unless they are necessary: if possible an everyday word should be used if this can be done without affecting the meaning of the sentence. Furthermore, technical terms should not be used in an attempt to impress non-technical readers – or even your teachers.

However, you should appreciate the value of the special words of your subject, if you can use them correctly. Unless you can define these words and use them with accuracy and precision, you are handicapped in all your studies. See *Prepare definitions*, p. 61.

You cannot understand any question in coursework or examinations unless you are certain of the meaning of every word used in the question. Only then can you plan a complete and correct answer.

Examiners expect you to spell correctly, understand, and if necessary define the technical terms used in talking and writing about your subject. Every subject has technical terms. For example:

British constitution: committee, constitution, government, politics, prorogation
Chemistry: asymmetry, desiccate, fluorine, potassium, separate, soluble
Geology: density, scenery, volcano
English literature: descriptive, lyric, narrative skill, novel
History: accession, dynasty, domestic, legislative
Music: bar, bass, concerto, note, octave, serenade, sonata, symphony.

Consider the technical terms you use. Can you define them?

The examiner was not impressed by the candidate who, in a general studies paper, spelt satellite in eight ways in one essay – even though the correct spelling was given in the question.

In English literature students are expected to spell correctly the names of characters in the set book. And all students of European history should be able to spell proper names: Disraeli, Victor Emmanuel, Napoleon, and Peel, for example.

ABBREVIATIONS

Avoid abbreviations if you can. Like complete words, they must be understood by your reader. Remember that abbreviations which are commonly used in one country may not be understood in another, and also that one abbreviation may have several meanings, so that even after referring to a dictionary of abbreviations your reader may still not know which meaning you intended. Any essential abbreviation should be written in full when it is first used, and immediately abbreviated in parenthesis. Make sure you are consistent in using abbreviations and in their punctuation.

Try to convey your meaning without using phrases from another language, or even abbreviations of such phrases. *Loc. cit.* (in the place cited), *op. cit.* (in the work cited), and *ibid.* (in the same work), like the words former and latter, may contribute to ambiguity. Even the abbreviations i.e. (*id est*: that is) and e.g. (*exempli gratia*: for example) are misused and, therefore, misunderstood by some people. Write namely, not *viz*; and about, not approximately, *circa, ca., c.,* or ∼ . The abbreviation etc. (*et cetera*: and other things), used at the end

Table 12 It pays to increase your word power

___

1   Prefer a short word to a long one unless the long word will serve your purpose better (see p. 49).
2   Consult a dictionary whenever you some across a word you do not understand.
3   Choose words that convey your meaning precisely: do not write words in quotation marks (inverted commas) to indicate that you do not mean quite what you say.
4   Show your understanding of the words you use by using them correctly, in context (see Tables 10 and 11).
5   Use technical terms only if these are necessary and will help you to communicate with the reader you have in mind.
6   Avoid abbreviations if you can.

___

of a list, conveys no additional information, except that the list is incomplete. It is better to write either for example or including immediately before the list.

These examples show the use of the full stop to indicate abbreviations. However, many abbreviations are not punctuated: for example, abbreviations that include the final letter of a word, such as Mr, Dr (an exception is nos., numbers); or acronyms, such as WHO (World Health Organization) and ISO (International Standards Organization). Note particularly that a full stop should not be used after a symbol for an SI unit (see International System of Units, Table 19, p. 78). Another rule is that an s should not be added to an abbreviation, except for nos. (numbers) and figs (figures in the sense of illustrations).

IMPROVE YOUR WRITING

Use a dictionary

Whenever you come across a word that you do not understand, consult a dictionary. You will find this interesting and it will help you to increase the number of words at your command (see Table 12).

Consult a dictionary

If necessary, consult a dictionary to help you to distinguish between: adverse and averse, affectation and affection, aggravate and irritate, all together and altogether, allusion and illusion, anticipate and expect, beside and besides, born and borne, breath and breathe, canon and cannon, canvas and canvass, childish and childlike, dependant and dependent, deficient and defective, deprecate and depreciate, device and devise, discreet and discrete, except and accept, economic and economical, farther and further, formally and formerly, effective and efficient, eligible and illegible and ineligible, exceedingly and excessively, historic and historical, human and humane, industrial and industrious, illusion and allusion, imperial and imperious, implicit and explicit, ingenious and ingenuous, interfere and intervene, lightening and lightning, loose and lose, luxuriant and luxurious, marshal and martial, masterly and masterful, moral and morale, notable and noticeable, populace and populous, practicable and practical, practice and practise, precede and proceed, prescribe and proscribe, recourse and resource, reverend and reverent, review and revue, sceptic and septic, seasonable and seasonal, stationary and stationery, suspect and surmise, urban and urbane.

Try writing pairs of sentences using each word correctly in context.

Understand the words used in questions

Consider carefully and make sure that you understand the precise meaning of each of the following words, used in questions: account, analyse, argue, comment, compare, consider, define, describe, discuss, essay, evaluate, evidence, explain, illustrate, list, opinion, outline, review, state, and summarize. Many marks are lost by students who do not think carefully about the words used in the question before they start their answer.

Make sure that you understand the question. Answer the question set (see p. 43). Respond to the precise wording of the question. The words used may tell you that the answer has to be in *a few words*, or *in your own words*, or *in full detail*. You may be asked to name *one . . .*, or to give *one* example of *. . .*, or to *assess* the relative importance of *. . .*, or to indicate *to what extent . . .*, or to state *how far . . .*

You will get little credit for recalling and writing out all your notes on the subject of the question, or for writing all you know about any subject, if what you write is not an answer to the question.

Prepare definitions

You may use a word in an appropriate context and yet have difficulty in defining it precisely. This is why examiners ask for definitions. When you have to define a word, note the points that must be included (as in a topic outline) and then write your definition.

In any definition, proceed from the general to the particular. That is to say, state the general class to which the thing to be defined belongs (for example, a *verb* is a word) and then the features that are peculiar to the thing defined (it is a word that indicates action). Your definition must be as simple as possible but it must apply to all instances of the thing defined and no others; and it may be followed by an example. See Table 34, p. 173.

Chapter 6

Using words

In a dictionary, each word is first explained and then used in appropriate contexts to make its several meanings clear. For words do not stand alone: each word gives meaning to and takes meaning from the sentence, so that there is more to the whole than might be expected from its parts.

WORDS IN CONTEXT

Some people have favourite words and phrases — such as, also, apparently, case, found, incidentally, in fact, make, occur, of, perhaps, quite, and show. The use of a word twice in the same sentence, or several times in the same paragraph, or many times on the same page, may interrupt the smooth flow of language, and writers usually try to avoid such undue repetition. But do not be afraid to repeat a word if necessary. The right word should not be replaced by a less apt word for the sake of what is called elegant variation. Moreover, you may choose to repeat a word to emphasize an important point.

The position of a word in a sentence should also reflect the emphasis you wish to put upon it. An important word may, for example, come near the beginning or near the end, and in either position it may help to link the ideas expressed in successive sentences.

The position of a word may transform the meaning of a sentence. The word *only* is well known for the trouble it may cause when it is out of place. Putting it in the wrong place is partly attributable to custom, but is also a sign of carelessness. It is worth taking the trouble to be unambiguous (see Table 13).

Table 13 Examples of the word *only* out of place

Extract	Meaning intended
The chemical was only manufactured in Europe.	The chemical was manufactured only in Europe.
The words no doubt should only be used when the idea of certainty is to be conveyed.	The words no doubt should be used only when the idea of certainty is to be conveyed.
I can only write well when I know what I want to say.	I can write well only when I know what I want to say.
It only works well for straightforward pieces of descriptive writing.	It works well only for straightforward pieces of descriptive writing.
She only made one journey which aroused the interest of detectives.	Only one of her journeys aroused the interest of detectives.
In this book those points of grammar only are discussed which will help you to ensure accuracy.	In this book only those points of grammar which will help you to ensure accuracy are discussed.

Consider the meaning of each of the following sentences. 'I only eat fish on Fridays.' 'I eat only fish on Fridays.' 'I eat fish only on Fridays.' 'I eat fish on Fridays only.' 'Only I eat fish on Fridays.' When you use the word *only*, are you sure the reader takes the meaning you intended?

The words *this*, *that*, and *it* (*he* or *she*) and *one*; *former* and *latter*; and *other* and *another*, must be used with care or ambiguity may result. If necessary a noun should be repeated.

In writing at school or college, except in reporting conversation, it is best to use standard language and to avoid colloquial language and slang.

Standard English: written language or language used formally.

Colloquial English: usually spoken English (or language used informally — as between close friends). Except in reporting speech, colloquial English should not be used in scholarly writing. In particular, do not use such contractions as don't (do not), it's (it is) or they're (they are), and won't (will not), in coursework or examinations.

Slang: highly colloquial language including new words or words used in a special sense.

Table 14 Avoid idiomatic expressions

Idiomatic expression	Meaning
explore every avenue	consider all possibilities
break new ground	start something new
it goes without saying	obviously
read between the lines	understand more than is said or written
in the pipeline	being prepared
work against time	try to finish in the time available

In his *Usage and Abusage: A Guide to Good English*, Eric Partridge (8th edn 1965, London, Hamish Hamilton) gives, as an example of the difference: man (standard); chap (colloquial); and bloke, guy, stiff and bozo (slang). If you are not sure whether or not a word is acceptable in scholarly writing, consult a dictionary (see p. 186). The words fellow, boy and man are standard English.

In writing at school or college it is also best to avoid clichés (see p. 48) and idiomatic expressions (see Table 14). In idiomatic expressions the words have a special meaning that might not be understood by some of your readers.

Ready-made phrases make less impact than does something new. They indicate that the writer has not troubled to choose words that convey the intended meaning precisely. In *Politics and the English Language* (in *Shooting an Elephant*, London, Secker & Warburg, p. 87) George Orwell wrote:

> As soon as certain topics are raised ... no one seems able to think of turns of speech that are not hackneyed: prose consists less and less of *words* chosen for the sake of their meaning, and more and more of *phrases* tacked together like the sections of a prefabricated hen-house.

In this way, people deny themselves the simple pleasure of putting their own thoughts into their own words. Instead, always:

> Open a new window,
> Open a new door.
> Travel a new highway
> That's never been tried before.
> > *Mame*, lyric by Jerry Herman (1966)

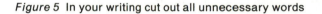

'I cut out only necessary words'

Figure 5 In your writing cut out all unnecessary words

SUPERFLUOUS WORDS

Using too many words is a more common fault in writing than using the wrong word; and while summarizing and qualifying phrases may help your readers (see also the remarks on comment words and connectives, p. 72), any unnecessary words can only confuse, distract and annoy. A well-constructed sentence should have neither too many words nor too few: each word should be there for a purpose (see Figure 5).

In his book *On the Art of Writing* (Cambridge University Press, 1916), Sir Arthur Quiller-Couch condemned jargon and gave the following advice. (a) Prefer transitive verbs and use them in the active voice. For example, write 'we obtained the following information' not 'the following information was obtained' (see also Table 17). (b) Prefer concrete nouns (things that you can touch and see) to abstract nouns. (c) Prefer the direct word to the circumlocution (see Tables 15 and 16).

Quiller-Couch listed words that should be used *sparingly and with care* by those who wish to avoid jargon: case, instance, character, nature, condition, persuasion, and degree. Other indicators of jargon are: area, angle, aspect, fact, field, level, situation, spectrum, time, and type (see Tables 5, 15 and 16). Of course there is nothing wrong with any of these words if you need them to convey your meaning.

Many introductory phrases and connectives can be deleted without altering the meaning of the sentence (see Tables 4 and 5). If you are in the habit of using such phrases, cut them out and your writing will be more direct, easier to read, and therefore more effective in conveying your meaning.

Circumlocution – verbosity – gobbledegook – surplusage – this habit of excess in the use of words, which makes communication more difficult than is necessary, is well established in the speech and writing of many people:

> Of all the Studies of men, nothing may be sooner obtain'd than this vicious abundance of *Phrase*, this trick of *Metaphors*, this volubility of *Tongue*, which makes so great a noise in the World. But I spend words in vain; for the evil is now so inveterate, that it is hard to know whom to *blame*, or where to begin to *reform*. We all value one another so much, upon this beautiful deceit; and labour for so long after it, in the years of our education: that we cannot but ever after think kinder of it, than it deserves.
>
> *The History of the Royal Society*, Thomas Sprat (1667)

Reasons for verbosity

Tautology, circumlocution, and verbosity arise from ignorance of the exact meaning of words. Also, people may use too many words, or too few, if they have not considered the difference between speech and writing.

> Human communication, it sometimes seems to me, involves an exaggerated amount of time. How briefly and to the point people always seem to speak on the stage or on the screen, while in real life we stumble from phrase to phrase with endless repetition.
>
> *Travels with My Aunt*, Graham Greene (1969)

Sometimes in conversation we use more words than would be needed in writing. We use words to separate important ideas; we repeat things for emphasis; and we correct ourselves as we talk – in an attempt to achieve greater precision. These things give the listener time to think. We hesitate and this gives us time to think.

Table 15 Circumlocution: the use of many words where fewer would be better

Circumlocution	Better English
Is this a temporary situation or is it permanent?	Is this temporary?
There was a large meaure of agreement.	Most people agreed.
not more than 20,000 to 25,000 words in length	no more than 25,000 words
a disproportionate number	too few, *or* few, *or* many, *or* too many (?)
ten metres in length	ten metres long
for a further period of fifteen years	for another fifteen years
the roads were limited in mileage	there were few roads
if at all possible	if possible
an oral presentation	a talk
on a dawn to dusk basis	from dawn to dusk
I would have thought	I think
I myself would hope	I hope
You are in fact quite correct	You are right
during the month of April	in April
in the field of medicine	in medicine
in the school environment	in schools
on the educational front	in education
at the pre-school level	the under-fives
Such is by no means the case.	This is not so.
The standard of English was poor in most cases.	The English of most candidates was poor.
In the case of the fifth question	In answering the fifth question
We are continuing to review the situation on a day to day basis.	We review the situation daily.
They are without any sanitary arrangements whatsoever.	There is no sanitation.
There is really somewhat of an obligation upon us	We ought
We are actually in the process of examining	We are examining
We are currently	We are
We are presently	We are
At the present time I am	I am
a lot of information condensed into a very little amount of space	a lot of information in a small space
Few candidates were not in a position to offer	Most candidates offered
No admittance to unauthorized personnel	No admittance

Table 16 Circumlocution: some phrases that should not be used if one word would be better

Circumlocution	Better English	Circumlocution	Better English
it would appear that	apparently	for the purpose of	for
owing to the fact that	because	aimed at	for
it is apparent therefore that	hence	if it is assumed that	if
		in the event that	if
in all other cases	otherwise	with the exception of	except
it may well be that	perhaps	entertainment value	fun
by the same token	similarly	in the vicinity of	near
with the result that	so	a sufficient number of	enough
in the process of building	building	a small number of	few
		a large number of	many
which goes under the name of	called	a large majority of	most
		a high degree of	much
has an ability to	can	a great deal of	much
is not in a position to	cannot	a number of	several
		a proportion of	some
in connection with	about	prior to	before
with regard to	about	if and when	if (or
in between	between	at a later date	when)
using a combination of	from	later on	later
in the nature of	like	a greater length of time	later longer
in order to	to		
in conjunction with	with	at the present time	
in spite of the fact that	although	at this precise moment in time	now now
to say nothing of	and	on a regular basis	
on account of the fact that	as	have been shown to be	regularly
		check on	are
make an adjustment to	adjust	take into consideration	check
afford an opportunity to	allow	come to the conclusion that	consider conclude
count-up	count	at that point in time	then
arrive at a decision	decide	after this has been done	then
give positive encouragement to	encourage	in this day and age	today
make an examination of	examine	on two separate occasions	twice
spell out in depth	explain	until such time as	until
bring to a conclusion	finish	in most cases	usually
conduct an investigation into	investigate	during the time that	while
		dusty in character	dusty
it must be remembered that	remember	somewhat costly	expensive
		of a reversible nature	reversible
seal off	seal		

Circumlocution	Better English	Circumlocution	Better English
undertake a study of	study	in view of the following	therefore
try out	try		
make an attempt to	try	are found to be in agreement	agree
proved to be	were		
at an early date	soon	open up	open

In conversation we use gestures and facial expressions. As we talk we see that the listener has grasped our meaning. We may therefore use fewer words than would be needed in writing.

In writing we must allow for the lack of direct contact with the reader. Meaning is conveyed by words alone, and we must use as many words as are needed to convey our thoughts precisely. On the one hand, therefore, more words may be necessary than in conversation. On the other hand, repetition can usually be avoided because the writer has time to plan and to revise. For the reader, necessary pauses come from punctuation marks and paragraph breaks.

> The writer ... suggests by turns of expression the emphasis and gestures of ordinary talk; uses vocabulary that is at once intelligible, interesting and evocative; and so varies his constructions that he avoids the effect of monotony. He gives coherence to speech, at the same time retaining certain of its characteristics. His immediate appeal is through the eye of the reader, but he does not forget the reader's ear.
>
> *The Best English*, G. H. Vallins
> (London, André Deutsch 1960, pp. 166–7)

Use words with which you are familiar and try to match your style to the occasion and to the needs of your readers. Write as you would speak but recognize that good spoken English is not the same as good written English. If a good talk is recorded and then typed, the reader may find that it is not good prose.

If they are prepared to take the trouble, most people should be able to write better than they can talk, because in writing there is more time for thought and there is the opportunity for revision.

Apart from failure to consider the difference between speech and writing, there are other reasons why people fill their writing with empty words. Some writers seem to think that restatement in longer words is explanation. Others are trying to make a little knowledge go a long way, or they may be trying to obscure meaning because they have nothing to say, or because they do not wish to commit themselves:

> 'Do, as a concession to my poor wits, Lord Darlington, just explain to me what you really mean.'
>
> 'I think I had better not, Duchess. Nowadays to be intelligible is to be found out.'
>
> *Lady Windermere's Fan*, Oscar Wilde (1892)

> only the wealthy, the capable, or the pretty can afford the luxury of saying right out just what they think, and blow the consequences.
>
> *Lieutenant Bones*, Edgar Wallace (1918)

Wordiness may also result from affectation — from the studied avoidance of simplicity — in the belief that Latin phrases, long words, and elaborate sentences appear learned.

> Foreign words and expressions ... are used to give an air of culture and elegance. The ends of sentences are saved from anti-climax by such resounding commonplaces as *greatly to be desired, cannot be left out of account, a development to be expected in the near future, deserving of serious consideration,* and *brought to a satisfactory conclusion.* Words like phenomenon, element, individual (as a noun), objective, categorical, effective, virtual, basic, primary, promote, constitute, exhibit, exploit, utilize, eliminate, liquidate, are used to dress up simple statement and give an air of scientific impartiality to biased judgements.
>
> *Politics and the English Language*, George Orwell (1950, p. 100)

Orwell recommends those who wish to use language as an instrument for expressing and not for concealing thought, to:

1 Be positive. Especially, avoid double negatives such as *not unlikely* (for possible) and *not unjustifiable.*
2 Never use a metaphor, simile or other figure of speech which you are used to seeing in print.
3 Never use a long word where a short one will do.
4 Never use a foreign phrase, a scientific word or a jargon word if you can think of an everyday English equivalent.
5 If it is possible to cut a word out, always cut it out.
6 Never use the passive where you can use the active.

Table 17 Examples of the use of the active and passive voice

Prefer the active voice to the . . .	passive voice
We all have to read a mass of papers.	A mass of papers has to be read.
I ask my colleagues and their staffs to . . .	My colleagues and their staffs are asked to . . .

The use of the passive enables the author to avoid the first person. The repeated use of *I* or *we* is undesirable, but some authors consider it impolite to refer to oneself directly and may go to great lengths (be verbose) in attempting to avoid doing so. Also, the editors of most scientific journals insist on the use of the passive: *Measurements were made*, not *I measured* or *We measured*. However, the first person is more direct and it can make a communication more personal and more forceful (Table 17).

The following memorandum on brevity was written by Winston Churchill in 1940 to the heads of all government departments.

To do our work, we all have to read a mass of papers. Nearly all of them are far too long. This wastes time, while energy has to be spent in looking for the essential points.

I ask my colleagues and their staffs to see to it that their Reports are shorter.

(i) The aim should be Reports which set out the main points in a series of short, crisp paragraphs.

(ii) If a Report relies on detailed analysis of some complicated factors, or on statistics, these should be set out in an Appendix.

(iii) Often the occasion is best met by submitting not a full-dress Report, but an *Aide-memoire* consisting of headings only, which can be expanded orally if needed.

(iv) Let us have an end of such phrases as these: 'It is also of importance to bear in mind the following considerations . . .', or 'Consideration should be given to the possibility of carrying into effect . . .'. Most of these woolly phrases are mere padding, which can be left out altogether, or replaced by a single word. Let us not shrink from using the short expressive phrase, even if it is conversational.

Reports drawn up on the lines I propose may at first sight seem rough as compared with the flat surface of officialese jargon. But the saving in time will be great, while the discipline of setting out the real points concisely will prove an aid to clearer thinking.

Simplicity is the outward sign of clarity of thought. Wordiness is therefore a reflection on a writer's thinking; and a means by which writers conceal meaning – perhaps even from themselves.

If men would only say what they have to say in plain terms how much more eloquent they would be.

On Style, Samuel Coleridge (1772–1834)

Anyone who wishes to become a good writer should endeavour, before he allows himself to be tempted by the more showy qualities, to be direct, simple, brief, vigorous and lucid.

The King's English, H. W. Fowler and F. G. Fowler (Oxford, Clarendon Press, 3rd edn, 1931, p. 11)

We shall be effective . . . as writers if we can say clearly, simply, and attractively just what we want to say and nothing more. If we really have something worth saying, then we are bound by the nature and necessities of our language to say it as simply as we can.

Our Language, Simeon Potter (Harmondsworth, Penguin Books, 1969, p. 103)

In practising an economy of words, do not make the mistake of using too few words. Include comment words (such as *even, dangerously, as expected,* and *unexpected*) and connecting words (such as *hence, however, moreover, nevertheless, on the contrary,* and *therefore*) to direct your reader's attention.

Table 18 Be direct, simple and brief

1   Use standard English (see pp. 63–4).
2   Express your meaning in your own words (see p. 64).
3   Prefer one word to a phrase if both convey the same meaning (see p. 68).
4   Include comment words and connecting words if they will help your readers to follow your train of thought (see p. 72).
5   Use enough words to ensure efficient communication – no more (see p. 72) and no fewer (see p. 73).

Do not pack important thoughts so closely that your reader has no time to grasp the full meaning of one before reading the next. Provide reminders when these are needed. Your subject should not be drowned in a sea of words, nor starved of the words needed to give it strength. The rule must be to use the number of words needed to convey a thought precisely (without ambiguity). Brevity must not be achieved at the expense of clarity, accuracy, interest, and coherence (see Table 18).

IMPROVE YOUR WRITING

Read to understand

Exercises in comprehension. Comprehension means understanding. Your understanding of any writing depends partly on the author's clarity of expression and partly on your vocabulary. An exercise in comprehension is an attempt, by asking questions, to find out whether or not you understand the words and phrases used in a particular context. The questions should be answered concisely and in your own words.

The exercise stimulates thought and provides opportunities for discussion. You learn not only about writing but also about your subject. Exercises in comprehension may therefore be set by other teachers − of geography, history, or science, for example − as well as by teachers of English.

Every question set in coursework and examinations is a test of your ability to understand. If you do not understand the exact meaning of the question you may answer the wrong question, or your answer may be incomplete.

Read to summarize

The ability to write précis and summaries will be useful when you take notes and when you wish to incorporate information and ideas, from any source, in one of your own compositions (see p. 36). As an employee you will need to select carefully if you wish, for example, to inform other people in the same organization of the relevant parts of an article or report. What you consider to be the essentials will depend upon why you are writing and for whom you are writing.

How to write a précis

Read the original more than once before you start your précis. Read first to make sure that you understand every sentence. Read again, using your judgement and selecting the main points: as you note these you are reconstructing the author's topic outline. Decide the author's purpose and then choose an effective heading for your précis. Keep this heading in mind as you make a rough draft based on your notes. Check your précis against the original, making sure that the writer of the original is acknowledged and accurately reported.

With practice you will grasp the essentials of a composition at first reading and you will find précis writing easier. The précis must be in good English, not in note form. The order of presentation should not be changed, unless the order is faulty. Remember that you are conveying the author's meaning accurately but in fewer words. Omit all figurative language or ornament, anything of secondary importance, and all digressions and superfluous words.

Regular practice in précis writing helps students to learn aspects of effective study: *careful reading* and *comprehension*, the *exercise of judgement* in *selecting* the essentials, and *accurate reporting*. Preparing a précis should also help students to learn more about selected aspects of their subject. Suitable exercises may therefore be set by teachers of other subjects, and not just by teachers of English.

Students may help themselves by practising the technique of précis writing. For example, you might try writing a précis of a leading article from a newspaper or of an article from a magazine or journal. Also, rewrite one of your own essays: try to reduce its length by 25 or 50 per cent.

How to write a summary

A summary differs from a précis in that it should be as short as possible. The summary of an article includes only the main points. It is like a topic outline but is written in complete sentences, not in note form. However, preparing a summary is a useful exercise for students, and you may find it useful to incorporate at appropriate points in your own notes (see p. 111) summaries of things you have read. Your own compositions in coursework and examinations will mostly be too short to require a summary.

The difference between a précis and a summary should be clear from the following examples: a précis of an extract from page 31 of *Human Biology*, a 'Made Simple' book published in 1981 by Heinemann, London; and a summary of the same extract.

Précis

Smoking or health?

Tobacco smoke contains many harmful chemicals, including the drug nicotine — on which smokers become dependent — and carbon monoxide which reduces the oxygen-carrying capacity of the blood. This causes smokers to become breathless quickly during exercise and increases the risk of a heart attack. The smoke also contains cancer-inducing chemicals and irritants that make smokers cough and cause bronchitis.

In Britain, more than twice as many smokers as non-smokers, aged thirty-five and over, die before the age of sixty-five. Since the danger to health first received publicity, many doctors have stopped smoking and deaths of doctors before the age of sixty-five, from diseases aggravated by smoking, have fallen by 21 per cent. But in the general population, who are not so well informed, deaths from smokers' diseases before the age of sixty-five have fallen by only 7 per cent.

Summary

Tobacco smoke contains harmful chemicals that cause drug-dependence, shortage of breath during exercise, heart attacks, smokers' cough, bronchitis, and cancer. Since this was established many people are living longer because they have stopped smoking.

Chapter 7

Using numbers, tables, and illustrations to complement your words

In some subjects, for example those concerned with the study of language and literature, it is usual to convey information and ideas using words alone. In other subjects numbers, tables and illustrations may be needed in most compositions to help you communicate your thoughts.

USE NUMBERS WHEN YOU CAN BE PRECISE

A politician may say that a fund will be established 'of *substantial* size and *adequate* coverage over a *considerable* period'. Vague words are used to express hopes when it is not possible to be precise.

Consider the meaning you wish to convey before you use the word *very* with an adverb (*very quickly*) or with an adjective (*very large*), and before you use adverbs (e.g. slowly) or adjectives (e.g. *small, appreciable, large,* and *heavy*) or modifying and intensifying words (e.g. *comparatively, exceptionally, extremely, fairly, quite, rather, really, relatively* and *unduly*). Vague statements will annoy the reader:

> Whenever anyone says I can do something soon I'll say to them, yes, I know all about that . . ., but when, when, when?
>
> *Key to the Door,* Alan Sillitoe (1969)

In your writing, instead of such vague words use numbers to make clear how many. Use numbers and appropriate units of measurement to indicate exact quantities: how far, how long, how much, how thick. Be precise when you can.

Except in scientific writing, numbers less than 100 are usually written in words: and symbols should be avoided. The number of the year should always be written in figures, and dates should be written *either* 20 January 1995, *or* 20th January 1995. Roman numerals may be used for the names of monarchs: Queen Elizabeth II or Queen Elizabeth the Second.

In writing, cardinal numbers (twenty-one to ninety-nine) and ordinal numbers (for example: twenty-first, one-hundred-and-first) should be hyphenated.

Always use words, not figures, at the beginning of a sentence. Use words for numbers one to nine, even in scientific writing, except before a symbol (6 m, but six metres) or percentage (6 per cent). Note also that two numbers should not be written together either as numerals or words, because ambiguity may result: write two 50 W lamps, not 2 50 W nor two fifty watt.

Decimals are indicated by a full stop on the line or, in some countries, by a comma. In scientific writing the comma should not, therefore, be used to break numbers above 999 into groups of three digits. With more than four digits, spaces should be left: 9999 but 10 000 and 999 999, etc. except that the numbers in a table must be in vertical alignment — which explains why a space is left in the numbers 4 937 and 8 510 in Table 20.

Because of possible confusion arising from differences between European and US usage, the words billion, trillion, and quadrillion should not be used.

Most countries have adopted the metric system of measurement and use the International System of Units (Système International d'Unités, abbreviated to SI: see Table 19). If it is necessary to use symbols, instead of words, the following rules apply. Leave a space between the number and the symbol (50 W and 20 °C). Do not put a full stop after the symbol unless it comes at the end of a sentence. And do not add an s to any symbol to make it plural (m = metre or metres; ms = millisecond or milliseconds).

USE TABLES AND ILLUSTRATIONS TO HELP YOU EXPLAIN

Tables and illustrations capture attention and should be used to emphasize important points. They should help you to communicate information or ideas clearly, concisely, forcefully, and quickly — with fewer words than would otherwise be needed.

Consider tables and illustrations as part of your composition — not as ornament. They should complement your writing. Do not add them at the end as if they were an afterthought. Instead, when planning a composition, consider how information or ideas can be

Table 19 International System of Units (SI units)

Quantity	Unit	Symbol
length	millimetre (0.001 m)	mm
	centimetre (0.01 m)	cm
	metre	m
	kilometre (1000 m)	km
area	square centimetre	cm²
	square metre	m²
	hectare	ha
volume	cubic centimetre	cm³
	cubic metre	m³
capacity	millilitre (0.001 l)	ml
	litre	l
mass	gram (0.001 kg)	g
	kilogram	kg
	tonne (1000 kg)	t
density	kilogram per cubic metre	kg/m³
time	second	s
	minute (60 s)	min
	hour (3600 s)	h
	day (86 400 s)	d
speed, velocity	metre per second	m/s
	kilometre per second	km/s
temperature (*t*)	degree Celsius	°C

Notes: The International System of Units includes *base units* (e.g. the metre, kilogram, and second); and *derived units* (e.g. centimetre and gram). The litre, tonne, minute, hour, day, and degree Celsius are recognized units outside the International System. The hectare is accepted temporarily in view of existing practice. In Britain the degree Celsius used to be called the degree centigrade. For further information on SI units, including units not shown in this table, see the British Standard BS 5555 or the identical International Standard ISO 1000.

best conveyed − to the readers you have in mind − in words, numbers, tables, or illustrations.

Information presented in one way (for example, in Table 20) should not also be presented in another way in the same composition (as it is in Figures 11 and 12, p. 86). Instead, include a table or illustration − depending on your purpose and the needs of the reader − but do not use both to convey the same information. By planning, you can avoid repetition and also ensure that in your composition each table and each illustration can be:

1 numbered;
2 arranged so that, if possible, it fits upright on the page;

3 placed near the relevant text, so that if possible the reader can look from one to the other without turning the page; and

4 referred to at least once in the text with, if necessary, cross-references included in other (usually later) parts of the same composition.

Tables

In a table words or numbers, or both, are arranged for easy reference, usually in columns. For example, a table of contents is a list of headings and page numbers, to help readers see how a long composition is organized and to help them find parts that may be of interest. Other tables are useful, especially in extended essays and project reports (see p. 133), because they allow you to provide additional relevant information, concisely, without interrupting the flow of words.

The tables in a composition should be numbered consecutively, be appropriately placed, and have clear and concise headings (see Table 19). The reader should be able to understand the tables without reading the text, but there should be at least one reference to each table in the text (as in the last sentence).

The first column on the left of a table is called the stub. This labels the horizontal rows of the table, indicating what the investigator has decided to study (called the independent variable). For example, in a table used to record numerical data or the results of the analysis of such data, the stub could state the times at which readings were taken – or the individuals, nations, or world regions selected for study (see Table 20).

The data or results recorded in other columns of a table, the values of which will depend on changes in the independent variable, indicate changes in dependent variables. There is one column for each dependent variable studied, as indicated by concise column headings – which must include units of measurement for every quantity shown. If there is no entry in any part of a table, this should be shown by three dots . . . and a footnote stating that no information is available. A nought should be used only for a zero reading.

Any necessary footnotes should be immediately below the table to which they apply, but there should be no other writing on the same page. Each footnote should be preceded by a letter or symbol (not by a number), which must also be included in the table to identify the entry to which the footnote refers (as in Table 20).

Table 20 The world: people and land

World region	Population (millions)		Surface area[a] (000s km²)
	1950	1990	
Africa	222	642	30 338
The Americas[b]	332	724	42 082
Asia[c]	1377	3113	27 580
Europe[c]	393	498	4 937
Oceania	12.6	26.5	8 510
Former USSR	180	289	22 402
World totals[d]	2517	5293	135 849

Notes:
[a] Including unproductive land
[b] Including Hawaii
[c] Former USSR shown separately
[d] All estimates from 1992 edition (published 1994) of *United Nations Demographic Year Book*, New York, United Nations.

If tables of data are necessary, for example in a report, these are best placed in an appendix so that they are readily available for reference but do not distract the readers' attention from your argument in the text.

Most text tables should be concise summaries (results of the analysis of data), to provide readers with just the information they need and to help you make a point. Whether the tables are in an appendix or in the text, horizontal and vertical ruled lines should be included only if they will help readers. In most text tables vertical lines are not needed (see Table 20).

Illustrations

Different kinds of illustrations, which may be photographs, drawings, or diagrams, are all called figures. They should be numbered consecutively, separately from the tables, and each one should have a concise caption or legend – immediately below the figure – so that the reader can understand the figure without reference to the text.

Photographs may be included in project reports. Otherwise, drawings or diagrams are more appropriate.

Line drawings are most likely to be used in practical reports, with each line intended as an accurate record of an observation. Because of this, preparing a line drawing is an aid to observation (see p. 13),

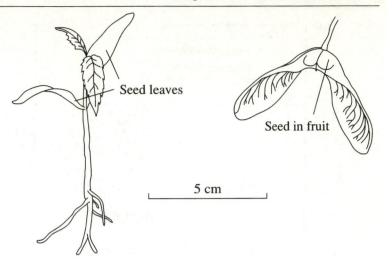

Seed leaves

Seed in fruit

5 cm

Figure 6 A line drawing: fruit and seedling of a maple tree, *Acer* sp.

and a completed drawing is a summary of observations (see Figure 6). If the proportions are to be correct the drawing must be to scale, and a scale should be marked on the drawing in metric units.

Instead of shading, in a line drawing effective labelling directs the reader's attention to different structures or parts. The labelling lines should be drawn by placing a pencil point on the thing to be labelled and, using a rule, drawing a straight line away from this point. Labelling lines should not cross one another, and should radiate from the drawing so that they are well spaced and the illustration as a whole (drawing and labelling) is well balanced. Arrowheads should not be used on labelling lines, because (a) it may not be clear whether the arrowhead ends on or points to the structure to be labelled, and (b) in many drawings and diagrams arrows are used for other purposes.

In a drawing, as in a photograph, three-dimensional objects are represented in two dimensions. The drawing represents things as they are seen at one time from one place. A drawing, therefore, may help the reader but it could be misleading. For many purposes a diagram is better.

Types of diagram used for presenting numerical data, or results of the analysis of such data, include the graph or line chart (Figure 7), the histogram (Figure 8), the column graph or vertical bar chart (Figure 9), the horizontal bar chart (Figure 10), the pictorial bar chart (Figure 11), and the circular graph or pie chart (Figure 12).

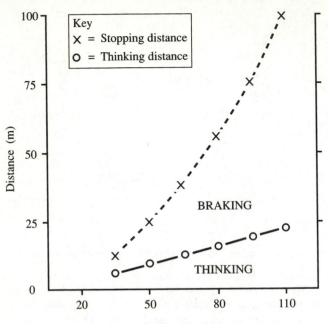

Figure 7 Graph or line chart: stopping distances for cars travelling at different speeds. Data from 1993 edition of *The Highway Code*, London HMSO

A graph or line chart shows how one thing varies relative to changes in another. The variable decided by the investigator, for example the times at which readings were taken (called the independent variable – see p. 79) must be plotted in relation to the horizontal axis. The other variable, over which the investigator has no control, and which depends on changes in the independent variable, is called the dependent variable (see p. 79) and is plotted in relation to the vertical axis. Only pure numbers are plotted.

The scales for the axes of a graph should normally start from zero; they should be chosen carefully and marked clearly. All numbers should be upright but the labelling of the scales should be parallel to the axes (as in Figure 7). Units of measurement must be stated. The diagram as a whole is the graph (line chart) and the lines on the graph, representing trends, even if they are best-fitting straight lines, are called curves.

Points on a graph are marked by symbols (usually by 0, × or +), which are also available to a printer as type and so in a publication could be included in legends.

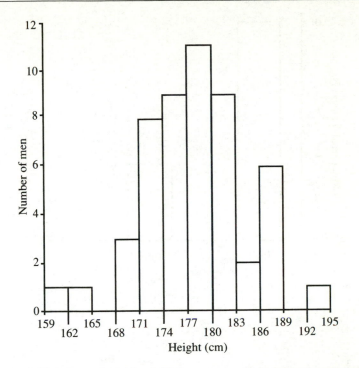

Figure 8 Histogram: heights of fifty-one men aged eighteen to twenty-five. Data from Harris, A. (1978), *Human Measurement*, London, Heinemann

Joining the points on a graph, by lines, may give a false impression; and to continue a line beyond the points on a graph may mislead the writer as well as the reader. A remark by Winston Churchill, made in another context, is appropriate: 'It is wise to look ahead but foolish to look further than you can see.'

To help the reader, if two or more graphs are to be compared they must be drawn to the same scale, and it is best if they can be placed side by side.

A histogram can be used to represent a frequency distribution in which the variation in the data is continuous (meaning that the observations recorded do not fall into distinct or discrete groups). As in a graph, the independent variable being studied (for example, the heights of people in Figure 8) is plotted in relation to the horizontal axis. The vertical column for each grouping interval shows the frequency of observations in that interval. Adjacent columns touch, indicating that the variation is continuous. On the horizontal axis the number on the left of each vertical column indicates the lowest measurement included in that grouping interval.

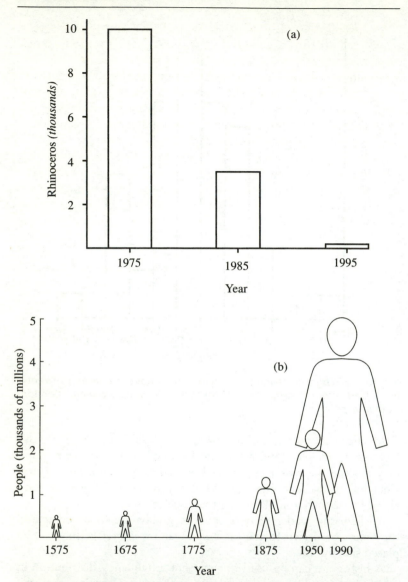

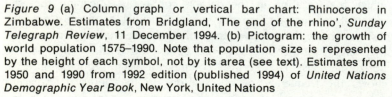

Figure 9 (a) Column graph or vertical bar chart: Rhinoceros in Zimbabwe. Estimates from Bridgland, 'The end of the rhino', *Sunday Telegraph Review*, 11 December 1994. (b) Pictogram: the growth of world population 1575–1990. Note that population size is represented by the height of each symbol, not by its area (see text). Estimates from 1950 and 1990 from 1992 edition (published 1994) of *United Nations Demographic Year Book*, New York, United Nations

A column graph, or vertical bar chart, can be used to represent a frequency distribution in which the variation in the data is discontinuous (the observations recorded do fall into discrete groups). As with line graphs and histograms, the variable being studied (the independent variable) is plotted in relation to the horizontal axis, and the length of a vertical column or bar indicates the frequency of observations in each group (the number or amounts of a dependent variable at different times or under different conditions).

Adjacent columns should be labelled separately and should not touch, emphasizing that the variation is discontinuous. As the data are discrete, there is no difficulty in assigning each observation to one group. For example, the number of children in a family must be a whole number. The columns must be rectangles (as in Figure 9a) because it is the height of the column, not its area, that corresponds to the quantity represented. Drawings should not be used as symbols, instead of columns (as in Figure 9b), because differences in the area of the drawings are likely to mislead the reader.

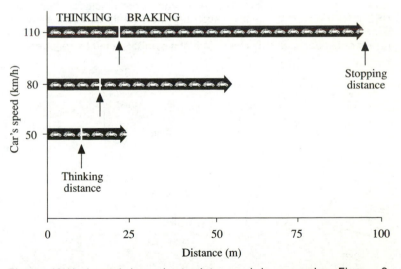

Figure 10 Horizontal bar chart: data used in preparing Figure 9, presented in a different way. These are the shortest stopping distances for alert drivers of cars with good brakes and tyres, on dry roads, when travelling at different speeds. Speed, decided by the driver, should be plotted in relation to the horizontal axis of a graph, but this chart is drawn on its side for visual effect – and greater impact. Distances are shown in metres and also in car lengths. Data from 1993 edition of The Highway Code, London, HMSO.

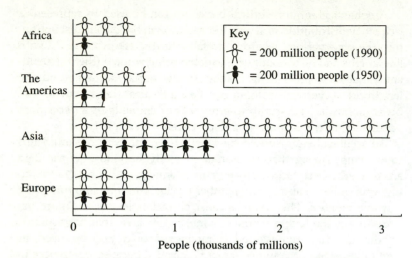

Figure 11 Pictorial bar chart: population growth in different world regions between 1950 and 1990 (based on data presented in Table 20). Note that the Americas include Hawaii, and Europe includes the former USSR. Note also that Oceania (Australia, New Zealand, and the Pacific islands), with a population of 26.5 million in 1990, could not be represented because only one-eighth of a symbol would be required

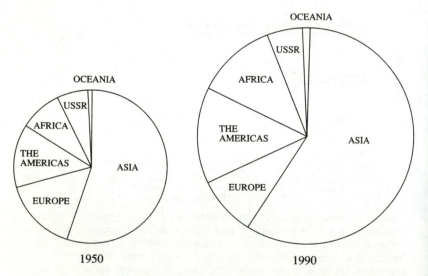

Figure 12 Circular graph or pie chart: where people lived in 1950 and 1990. The difference in area of these two charts represents the doubling of the world population (see Table 20)

In non-technical writing the bar chart may be drawn on its side (with the dependent variable represented on the horizontal axis) if horizontal bars are more appropriate, make more impact, and so help to convey a message more effectively (see Figure 10). In a pictorial bar chart (Figure 11) the bars must be replaced by identical symbols. A bar chart can also be used to show how one or more things vary in relation to another when one of the variables is not numerical (see Figure 20, p. 132).

If symbols or different kinds of shading are used in a diagram, a key must be provided — preferably as part of the diagram (as in Figure 11) rather than in the legend.

In a circular graph or a pie chart, slices of the pie are arranged in order, clockwise — starting at noon — from largest to smallest, with each slice representing a fraction of 360°. If two pie charts are to be compared the slices in the second should be arranged in the same order as in the first (as in Figure 12); and differences in the area of the pies may be used to indicate differences in sample size.

Some diagrams are not drawn to scale. Each line is not intended as an accurate record: it is the diagram as a whole that provides a useful summary of observations or ideas (see Figure 17 on p. 111).

If a diagram is drawn to scale it may convey information more accurately than a photograph or drawing of the same subject. On such a diagram, a scale bar must be included (see Figure 13); and on a map there must also be an arrow indicating north (see Figure 14); and all diagrams that are to be compared must be drawn to the same scale.

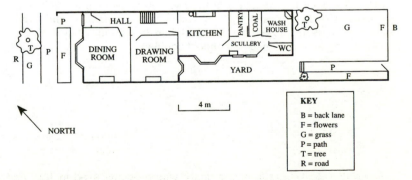

Figure 13 A diagram drawn to scale: ground-floor plan of an Edwardian terraced house built in Kingston upon Hull, England, in 1903

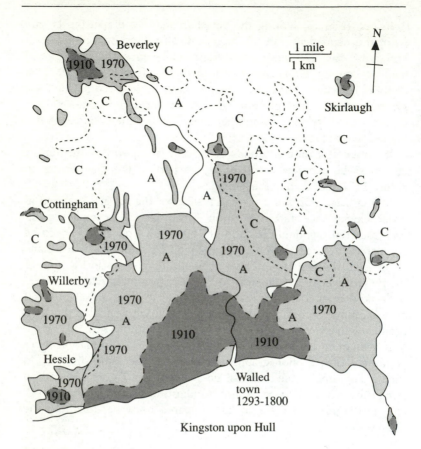

Figure 14 A diagram drawn to scale: map of Kingston upon Hull, England, showing the boundary of the new town, founded in 1293, and the boundaries in 1920 and 1970. A = alluvium; C = boulder clay. The population in 1970 was almost identical with that in 1921 but in these fifty years the area occupied had almost doubled

Chapter 8

Helping your readers

By making things easy for your readers, you help yourself to convey information and ideas. You should therefore find out as much as you can about your readers and try to match your vocabulary and style of writing to their needs. This is easiest if you are a student writing for one reader, or an employee writing to a colleague.

Try to anticipate your readers' difficulties so that your writing can be understood at first reading by all those for whom it is intended.

Provide an informative title and, if appropriate, use headings and subheadings as signposts. Present information in an effective order; include all essential steps in any argument; give sufficient evidence in support of anything new; give examples, and explain why any point is particularly important. No statement should be self-evident, but be as explicit as is necessary. Do not leave your readers to work out the implications of any statement. Help them to appreciate the connection between sentences and paragraphs. Sometimes a word or phrase is enough; sometimes much more explanation is required.

Try not to mislead your readers. Make clear any assumptions underlying your arguments, because if these were incorrect your conclusions might also be incorrect. Take care that any assumptions, conjectures, or possibilities are not later referred to as if they were facts. Words to watch, because they may introduce an opinion, are *obviously*, *surely*, and *of course* (see also Table 12).

Fulfil your readers' expectations. For example, follow the words *not only* by *but also*; *whether* by *or*; *on the one hand* by *on the other hand*; and *first(ly)* by *second*, *third*, etc. If you list items, mention all or none of them in the sentences that follow: if only some are mentioned, your readers may wonder about the others when they should be thinking about your next topic.

WRITE FOR EASY READING

Your writing should be appropriate to the subject, to the needs of your readers and to the occasion. Convey your thoughts clearly, accurately and impartially so that your readers take your meaning and always feel at ease.

How to begin

If you know what you wish to communicate but have difficulty in getting started, look at the opening sentences of similar compositions by other people. You might begin, for example, with a question or with an answer to one of your readers' six questions (see p. 29). The best starting point, for the subject and for your readers, will usually become apparent as you prepare your topic outline (see pp. 30–5). However, it is better to get started than to spend too much time trying to think of the most effective beginning. The only rules are: (a) leave no doubt about the purpose and scope of the composition – if this is not clear from the title – and in coursework and examinations make clear that you have begun to answer the question; (b) make your first paragraph short and to the point (see Emphasis, p. 91); and (c) start with things that you expect your readers to know and build on this foundation.

Control

Try to maintain the momentum of your writing. Do not dwell for too long on any topic, therefore, and make the connection between paragraphs clear. Apply the test of relevance to everything. Make sure that every word or phrase is appropriate to its context and that every sentence conveys a whole thought.

Good headings (see p. 30) and paragraph breaks help the reader along – but only if the headings and paragraphs are in an effective sequence that is obvious to the reader. Keeping control, therefore, depends upon your knowledge of the subject and upon careful planning (see p. 30) that enables you to deal fully with each topic in one place and to present your thoughts in an appropriate, ordered, and interesting way.

Emphasis

In speech, emphasis is achieved mainly by inflexions of the voice. In writing, mark in your topic outline the points you wish to emphasize, so that you can ensure they are sufficiently emphasized in your finished composition. There are many ways in which, without the sound of your voice, you can draw a reader's attention to parts of a composition, particular sentences in a paragraph, and selected words in a sentence.

The title and any headings and subheadings serve to emphasize the purpose of the whole and its parts. See pp. 30 and 89.

Emphasis is important in all writing and is present whether or not the writer is in control. But a writer, to use emphasis effectively, must know how to make important points stand out from the supporting detail.

Devote one paragraph to each topic. Paragraphs are units of thought and will therefore vary in length (see p. 34). However, if the topics are of comparable importance, you might expect to write paragraphs of similar length.

Plan effective diagrams if these will help you to convey the essential points of your composition (see p. 77), or if they are necessary to enable you to convey information that cannot be conveyed by words alone.

Beginnings and endings are most important. The first and last paragraphs (the introduction and conclusion − see pp. 90 and 95) are those to which readers pay most attention. The most important words in each paragraph are the first words (so miss out unnecessary introductory phrases − see Tables 4 and 5) and the last words (so end each paragraph effectively).

The most important words in a sentence, for emphasis, come at the beginning and at the end. The first words direct the reader's attention. The writer may use the same words to convey the same information and yet affect the reader differently, because the words that come first are emphasized. For example:

The first men on the moon were two United States astronauts, Neil Armstrong and Edward Aldrin.

Two United States astronauts, Neil Armstrong and Edward Aldrin, were the first men on the moon.

Neil Armstrong and Edward Aldrin, two United States astronauts, were the first men on the moon.

Asides, within a sentence, may be marked — according to the importance you place upon them — by commas, dashes, or parentheses (as in this sentence). (See also dashes and parentheses, p. 176.)

You may underline words in your topic outline or in your notes to draw attention to the most important points, but in a composition emphasis should normally be achieved without underlining. Underline only the words which, in books, would be printed in italics: conjunctions such as <u>but</u>, <u>and</u>, <u>either</u> ... <u>or</u>, and <u>neither</u> ... <u>nor</u>, when used — as in many examination questions — to make an important distinction or contrast; the titles of books, plays and poems (for example, <u>Hamlet</u> the play, but Hamlet the man); the names of newspapers, magazines and journals (for example, <u>The Times</u>); the scientific names of genera (for example, <u>Homo</u>) and of species (for example, <u>Homo sapiens</u>); and words from a foreign language which are used in English but not accepted as English words (for example, <u>modus operandi</u> and <u>in loco parentis</u>).

Leave out anything that is irrelevant, not only because irrelevant material wastes everyone's time but also because you must take care not to draw the reader's attention away from relevant material. Use more forceful language for important points than for the supporting detail. Repeat important words.

Items of comparable importance may be emphasized *by* repeating an introductory word (as in this sentence), *by* numbering (as on p. 93), or *by* indentation (see the quotations on p. 95). However, if a sentence or paragraph is well balanced, so that it reads well, emphasis will fall naturally on each part.

Long, involved sentences may indicate that you have not thought sufficiently about what you wish to say. However, if it is properly constructed, a long sentence may be easier to read than a succession of short ones. There is no rule that a sentence, when read aloud, should be read in one breath.

For the beginner, short sentences are easiest to write and easiest to read, but good prose is seldom written entirely in short sentences. Sentences vary in length. Short sentences are effective for introducing a new topic (as in two of the preceding twelve paragraphs), long sentences for developing a point, and short ones for emphasizing each step in an argument or, as in the quotation that follows, for bringing things to a striking conclusion.

'If you really want to know,' said Mr Shaw with a sly twinkle, 'I think that he who was so willing and able to prove that what was, was not, would be equally able and willing to make a case for thinking that what was not, was, if it suited his purpose.' Ernest was very much taken aback.

The Way of All Flesh, Samuel Butler (1903)

The breaks between sentences give time for thought; Rudolph Flesch (1962), in *The Art of Plain Talk* (London and New York, Collier-Macmillan), grades writing, according to *average* sentence length, as very easy to read (less than 10 words), difficult (more than 20 words) and very difficult (more than 30 words). Accept this as a guide, and match your sentence length to the needs of your readers.

Rhythm

Well-written prose has a varied rhythm that contrasts with the strict metred rhythm of verse, and yet contributes to the flow of words in a sentence. With the flow of carefully arranged thoughts in success-ive sentences, this helps to make a passage interesting and easy to read. Rhythm may give emphasis and help to present shades of meaning.

Use punctuation marks to clarify meaning and to contribute to the smooth flow of language. Effective prose usually sounds well, and a good test of your writing is to read it aloud to see if it is easy to read. E. S. McCartney (1953), in his *Recurrent Maladies of Scholarly Writing* (Ann Arbor, University of Michigan Press), suggests that writers with a feeling for euphony (the sounds of words) try not to offend the ear:

1 by unintentional alliteration, as in *rather regularly radial;*
2 by the grating repetition of s, as in *such a sense of success;*
3 by adding s to a word that does not require it, such as *toward* and *forward* (but the s may be needed to make the sentence easier to read);
4 by the repetition of syllables, as in *appropriate approach;*
5 by the repetition of sound, as in *found around;*
6 by the repetition of cognate forms in different parts of speech, as in a *locality located,* and *except for rare exceptions;* and
7 by repeating a word with a change of meaning, as in a *point to point out.*

Style

You cannot add style to writing, as a final polish, because it is part of effective prose. Jonathan Swift defined style as *proper words in proper places*, and Matthew Arnold considered that the secret of style is *to have something to say and to say it as simply as you can*.

R. Graves and A. Hodge (1947), in *The Reader over Your Shoulder* (London, Cape), suggest that the prose best suited to the present day should be:

1 Cleared of encumbrances for quick reading; that is, without unnecessary ornament, irrelevancy, illogicality, ambiguity, repetition, circumlocution, obscurity of reference.
2 Properly laid out; that is, with each sentence a single step and each paragraph a complete stage in the argument or narrative; with each idea in its right place in the sequence, and none missing; with all connections properly made.
3 Written in the first place for silent reading, but with consideration for euphony if read aloud.
4 Consistent in use of language; considerate of the possible limitations of the reader's knowledge; with no indulgence of personal caprice nor any attempt to improve on sincere statement by rhetorical artifice.

The need for careful planning is emphasized in these notes on style, and in Georges de Buffon's address to the Académie Française in 1703:

This plan is not indeed the style, but it is the foundation; it supports the style, directs it, governs its movement, and subjects it to law. Without a plan, the best writer will lose his way. His pen will run on unguided and by hazard will make uncertain strokes and incorrect figures. Style is but the order and the movement that one gives to one's thoughts.

A good style depends upon your intelligence, imagination and good taste; upon sincerity, modesty and careful planning. Rhythm, while not essential, will make for easier reading, and badly constructed sentences may irritate readers and make them less receptive to your message.

How to conclude

Your conclusion must be decided before you start to write (see p. 31); and in a short composition your last paragraph should not normally be a summary (see p. 35). Its topic may be the last main point in an argument, upon which you rest your case. Or you may speculate about the future course of events. Just as it is helpful to consider how other writers begin (see p. 90), so you can note how others bring their compositions to a close.

However, the end of your composition is your conclusion and should follow naturally from the preceding paragraphs. It should not take your assessor completely by surprise: there should not be a sting in the tail.

CAPTURE AND HOLD YOUR READER'S INTEREST

A novelist, whose business is words, must quickly capture and hold the reader's interest. Great care is taken over the choice and use of words. Consider, for example, the first paragraph of a successful novel:

> He rode into our valley in the summer of '89. I was a kid then, barely topping the backboard of father's old chuckwagon. I was on the upper rail of our small corral, soaking in the late afternoon sun, when I saw him far down the road where it swung into the valley from the open plain beyond.
>
> *Shane*, Jack Schaeffer (1954)

The first two words capture the reader's attention. The first sentence (in ten short words) tells what the story is about; it begins to answer the reader's questions – who, where, and when? The first paragraph tells that the story will be told as it affected the life of a small boy. No word is superfluous. Each one plays a part in setting the scene.

Note how interest is maintained in a newspaper report: by reference to familiar things, and by examples, anecdotes and analogies. Harold Evans in *Newsman's English*, Vol. 1 (London, Heinemann, 1972, p. 206) emphasizes that:

> Newspapers are short of space and their readers are short of time. The language must be concise, emphatic and to the point. Every word must be understood by the ordinary man, every sentence must be clear at a glance, and every story must say something about people.

Table 21 Write for easy reading

1   Decide what your readers need to know (see p. 28)
2   In your topic outline mark the points you will emphasise (see p. 31)
3   Approach your readers through their interests rather than your own (see p. 26)
4   Start with things you expect your readers to know (see p. 90)
5   Try to anticipate your readers' difficulties so that you can provide sufficient explanation, an analogy, or an example.
6   Keep to the point: try not to mislead your readers, and fulfil their expectations (see p. 89).
7   Match your average sentence length to the needs of the readers you have in mind (see p. 93).
8   Use punctuation marks to contribute to clarity and the smooth flow of language (see Appendix 3).
9   Remember that too many long words, long sentences, and long paragraphs, make it harder for the writer to maintain control – and make for hard reading.
10 Check that your composition sounds well when read aloud.

IMPROVE YOUR WRITING

Make your writing interesting

Write for easy reading (see Table 21). Approach your readers through their interests rather than your own. Remember that people are most interested in themselves, in other people, and in things as they affect people.

Newsman's English includes a number of editing exercises in which Evans removes superfluous words and rearranges the information to make each story more direct and more interesting to the reader.

To maintain interest, you must present information at a proper pace. If readers understand they will want to move quickly to the point. However, they must understand every word, every statement, and every step in any argument; for if they must consult a dictionary or read a sentence twice, to confirm that they have taken the right meaning, their attention may be lost.

Use comment words and connecting words (see p. 72) to help your reader to move smoothly from one thought to the next. Readers are directed away from your explanation or argument by anything that is not relevant, by unnecessary detail, by the explanation of the obvious (but see p. 121), or by needless repetition.

When anything is repeated, for emphasis or to help to clarify a difficult point, use a phrase such as *that is to say* or *in other words*. Otherwise, after studying both sentences to make sure that their meaning is the same, readers may still wonder if they have failed to appreciate some difference.

Use good English

Mistakes in grammar make writing inaccurate, imprecise and ambiguous. Grammar (the art of speaking, reading and writing correctly) is not therefore something that can be ignored: it may be acquired subconsciously by those who speak well and read good prose; or it may be learned with effort from a teacher of English or by studying a textbook on the English language – and by reading good prose.

Read good English

In starting to play any game, it is a good idea to watch an expert. Similarly, in learning to write effectively, it is helpful to study the technique of the successful writer.

Evelyn Waugh (see also p. 26) advised a young writer to read the works of sixteenth-, seventeenth- and nineteenth-century authors. W. Somerset Maugham, in *The Summing Up* (1938), commends the prose of John Dryden (1631–1700), Joseph Addison (1672–1719), Jonathan Swift (1667–1745), William Hazlitt (1778–1830), John Henry Newman (1801–90), and Matthew Arnold (1822–88). Maugham (see also pp. 25–6) considers the two most important qualities in writing to be clarity and simplicity, but regrets that:

> English prose is elaborate rather than simple. It was not always so. Nothing could be more racy, straightforward, and alive than the prose of Shakespeare; . . . To my mind King James's Bible has had a harmful influence. . . . There are passages of a simplicity that is deeply moving. But it is an oriental book. Its alien imagery has nothing to do with us. Those hyperboles, those luscious metaphors, are foreign to our genius.

Some of the most successful British and American writers, in every age, have expressed themselves clearly and simply. Francis Bacon (1561–1626) in *Of Studies*, an essay, wrote:

> Read not to contradict and confute, nor to believe and take for granted, nor to find talk and discourse, but to weigh and

consider. . . . some books are to be read only in parts; others to be read but not curiously; and some few to be read wholly, and with diligence and attention.

In *As You Like It*, written in 1601, William Shakespeare wrote some of the best-known lines in the English language, in words that are still easily understood by all English-speaking people:

> All the world's a stage,
> And all the men and women merely players:
> They have their exits, and their entrances;
> And one man in his time plays many parts,
> His acts being in seven ages. At first . . .

Joseph Addison (1672–1719) in *A Citizen's Diary*, an essay, gave clear advice that is still easy to read and worth considering:

> I would, however, recommend to every one of my readers, the keeping a journal of their lives for one week, and setting down punctually their whole series of employment during that space of time. This kind of examination would give them a true state of themselves and incline them to consider seriously what they are about.

In *Robinson Crusoe*, the first English novel, published in 1719, Daniel Defoe wrote one of the best-known passages in English prose. Note the clear, direct and simple style:

> One day about noon going towards my boat, I was exceedingly surprised with the print of a man's naked foot on the shore, which was very plain to be seen in the sand. I stood like one thunderstruck, or as if I had seen an apparition.

Thomas Jefferson (1743–1826) wrote The Declaration of Independence of the United States of America, which begins:

> When in the Course of human events, it becomes necessary for one people to dissolve the political bands, which have connected them with another, and to assume among the powers of the earth, the separate and equal station to which the Laws of Nature and of Nature's God entitle them, a decent respect to the opinions of mankind requires that they should declare the causes which impel them to the separation.

'. . . the print of a man's naked foot . . . in the sand. I stood like one thunderstruck . . .'

Figure 15 To write well most people need to be left alone, free from distraction and with time for thought

The continuing appeal of the Declaration is due not only to its expression of the feelings of a people but also to Jefferson's clear and simple style.

William Hazlitt (1778–1830) in an essay *On the Ignorance of the Learned* wrote concisely and gave good advice to students.

> It is better to be able neither to read nor write than to be able to do nothing else. . . . Learning is, in too many cases, but a foil to common sense; a substitute for true knowledge. Books are less often made use of as 'spectacles' to look at nature with, than as blinds to keep out its strong light and shifting scenery from weak eyes and indolent dispositions.

Robert Louis Stephenson (1850–94) in *An Apology for Idlers*, an essay, emphasized the need for relaxation and the importance of everyday experiences.

> I have attended a good many lectures in my time. I still remember that the spinning of a top is a case of Kinetic Stability. I still

remember that Emphyteusis is not a disease, nor Stillicide a crime. But though I would not willingly part with such scraps of science, I do not set the same store by them as by certain other odds and ends that I came by in the open street.

Sir Arthur Bryant wrote a weekly Note Book in the *Illustrated London News* for more than thirty years. He wrote in clear and simple English; and in *The Lion and the Unicorn* (London, Collins, 1969, p. 15) he emphasized that the successful author must capture the reader's interest.

> If anyone wonders why my column in the *Illustrated London News* has any readers, I can only suggest the answer King Charles II gave when asked to explain how a particularly stupid clergyman, whom he had made a bishop, had converted his flock from dissent to orthodoxy: 'I suppose his sort of nonsense suits their sort of nonsense!'

Young writers, still developing a style of their own, will find clear, simple, and straightforward prose in, for example, books by Samuel Butler (see p. 93), Winston Churchill (see pp. 3 and 71), Robert Graves (see pp. 15 and 94), George Orwell (see p. 64), Dorothy L. Sayers (see p. 2), and H. G. Wells (see p. 16).

Read for pleasure. Without effort, as a result, you will find that your writing improves. Read widely, and you will find that successful authors do not waste words.

> Mr Stevens sat with his map on his knees, because he liked to pick out the distant church spires and name the clustering houses. He liked to find on the map the streams he would cross before they came in sight. He was fond of maps, and had learnt to read them well. They appealed to him because of the endless pleasure they offered his imagination, the picture they showed him of a country built up through the romantic casualness of centuries.
>
> *The Fortnight in September*, R. C. Sherriff (1931)

Just as the way we speak is influenced by the speech we hear, so our writing is influenced by the prose we read. The King James I Bible had a profound effect on speech and writing when it was the staple literature of English-speaking people, just as our daily newspapers do now. Most people read newspapers, and some read nothing else. Journalists and broadcasters use the English of today and may have an untold influence on the development of our language.

Read good newspapers

Readers of newspapers look first for things that are of interest; and they read only things that they can understand. Different newspapers are written to appeal to people with different views on politics; or to convert readers to a particular point of view. They are also intended to be understood by people who differ in intelligence. Look carefully at different newspapers to see if you can detect their political bias. In papers that you think are for more intelligent or better-educated readers what do you notice about the length of paragraphs, sentences, and words in comparison with papers written for less intelligent readers?

Because your vocabulary and style of writing are influenced by the things you read, it is best to read a good newspaper. Study the technique of journalists who write well, in feature articles and in leading articles especially, to see how to capture your readers' attention, how to inform, how to express a point of view, how to persuade, how to match your writing to the needs of your readers, and how to write a clear, concise, vigorous, and vivid prose.

However, it is a mistake to try to copy someone else's style. There is no one correct way to write, because the way you put words together to convey meaning reflects your personality and feeling for words.

Leonard was trying to form his style on Ruskin: he understood him to be the greatest master of English Prose. He read forward steadily, occasionally making a few notes.

'Let us consider a little each of these characters in succession, and first (for of the shafts enough has been said already), what is very peculiar to this church – its luminousness.'

Was there anything to be learnt from this fine sentence? Could he adapt it to the needs of daily life? Could he introduce it, with modifications, when he next wrote a letter to his brother, the lay reader? For example:

'Let us consider a little each of these characters in succession, and first (for of the absence of ventilation enough has been said already), what is very peculiar to this flat – its obscurity.'

Something told him that the modification would not do, and that something, had he known it, was the spirit of English Prose. 'My flat is dark as well as stuffy.' Those were the words for him.

Howards End, E. M. Forster (1910)

Chapter 9

Finding information

THINK BEFORE YOU READ

Whenever you have to write, first think about the subject. Make sure you understand the title, the question you must answer, or the terms of reference (see p. 127). Ask the questions recommended on page 29. Get as far as you can, preparing your topic outline, before you look for other sources of information. Otherwise you will find an original approach to the subject more difficult.

Making a start with your topic outline will also help you to recognize gaps in your knowledge. Then you can look for just the information you require (see Table 22). But remember that the time you spend on the search for additional information must be carefully related to the total time available for thinking, planning, writing, and revising (see Figure 16, p. 109).

The following extracts are from an address on reading, delivered at Manchester in 1903, by John Lubbock.

> No one can read a good and interesting book for an hour without being better for it; happier and better, not merely for the moment, but the memory remains . . .
>
> It is indeed most important that those who use a library should use it wisely. Do we make the most of our opportunities? It is a great mistake to imagine that everyone knows how to read. On the contrary, I should say that few do so. Two things have to be considered: how to read and what to read.

USE YOUR LIBRARY

In any library, if you have difficulty in finding information on any

Table 22 Some sources of information

Activities	Sources
Thinking	Personal observation Private records
Talking	Asking questions Unpublished records
Writing	Correspondence
Reading	Dictionaries Encyclopaedias Handbooks and standards Directories Books Journals and magazines Newspapers Photographs Maps Sound recordings, tape–slide programmes Films and videos Computer-assisted learning materials Computer-based information retrieval systems Interactive multimedia

subject ask a librarian for help. The librarian can also show you how to reserve a book that has been borrowed by another reader, or how to obtain a book on inter-library loan. However, if you are not sure what information you are looking for, ask a lecturer or tutor for further advice on where to begin your reading.

Refer to a good *dictionary* (see p. 186) if you are uncertain of the status, spelling, pronunciation, or meaning of any word. Remember also that there are specialized dictionaries of, for example, the technical terms used in your subjects. And there are dictionaries of abbreviations (see p. 58) and of idiomatic expressions (see Table 14, p. 64).

Encyclopaedias are a good starting point for anyone coming new to a subject. The best-known, most authoritative, and most detailed encyclopaedias in the English language include the multi-volume *Encyclopaedia Britannica* and *Hutchinson's Encyclopaedia* in one volume.

Entries in an encyclopaedia are in alphabetical order. Each entry is written by an expert on the subject. Information and ideas are presented simply, clearly, and concisely, like a short essay. Always look at the index as well as the entry; this may lead you to other relevant entries.

Handbooks are concise reference books for day-to-day use (see further reading: Appendix 4 p. 186). Each handbook provides information on one subject.

Directories provide names and addresses and sometimes other information. The best known are the telephone directories; but there are other directories of the names of trades, industries, and organizations. You should know of such lists of authors and titles as *Books in Print* (published in the United States) and *Whitaker's Books in Print* (published in Britain). In these you can see whether or not a book that you require is in print; or whether or not the copy you have is the latest edition (see p. 108).

Books in a library are arranged on the shelves according to subject, so you might expect to be able to see all the books on your subject stocked by any library simply by looking on the shelves. There are three main reasons why this is not possible. First, some books will be on loan or being used in the library by other students. Second, books on one subject may be stored on different shelves and in different parts of the library. For example, some books on fungi will be shelved with other books on biology or botany, but others may be with books on agriculture, medicine, brewing, timber decay, or stored products – depending on their titles and contents. Third, the librarian has to decide where to place each book that is likely to be of interest to students taking interdisciplinary courses.

In classifying books according to subject, different libraries use different classification systems (see Table 23). In the Dewey Decimal System, for example, there are ten classes (numbered 000 to 900 in Table 23). In each class there are nine divisions (for example, 910, 920 and 930 in Table 23). Books are further classified within each division; and the full subject classification number of each book (the book or shelf number) is printed on its spine.

If you would like to know which books on a particular subject are stocked by a library, you must know how the books are classified in that library, and how to use the subject index. If you are looking for a particular book, you must know the name of the author, the title, or the book number. You can then find where the book is shelved by consulting the author and title catalogue, or the classified catalogue. These may be on index cards or microfiche, or may be

Table 23 Three systems used for classifying books in libraries

The ten classes of the Dewey Decimal System		Universal Decimal System	Library of Congress System
000	General works	0	A
	Reference books (030)	03	AE
100	Philosophy	1	B
	Psychology (150)	15	BF
200	Religion	2	BL
300	Social sciences	3	H
400	Languages	4	P
500	Pure sciences	5	Q
600	Applied sciences	6	
700	The Arts	7	N
800	Literature	8	P
900	Geography (910)	91	G
	Biography (920)	92	CT
	History (930)	93	C

computer-based. You are advised to read any leaflets available in the library explaining how to use the catalogues.

Most university libraries have computer-based online public-access catalogues, accessed from computer terminals – from which it may also be possible to search the catalogues of other university libraries and those of some other major public libraries, linked in a network.

To access such a computer-based catalogue, read the printed instructions displayed next to the computer terminal; and then read the instructions on the screen at each stage of your catalogue search. You may choose to search by keyword, author's or editor's name, book's title, class number, or the name of an organization (an originator).

If you need information on a topic, but do not know the author or title of a particular book, you can enter one or more keywords. By this keyword search (a) you may be able to locate a book even if you do not have its complete title, or other bibliographic details, and (b) you can find books on a particular subject (but you will locate only books with titles that include the keywords you have used – so a subject search is better).

Books are listed alphabetically according to the names of their authors or editors, or the organizations that produced them (the originator: for example, a government department or society). When you find the catalogue entry for any book, this will include complete bibliographic details (see p. 110) and also the book's subject classification number.

If the catalogues are accessed from a computer terminal, other information displayed will include: the number of copies of the book in stock; whether or not the book can be borrowed; and, if it is on loan, when it is due to be returned.

Signposts on library floor plans, and on the shelves, include the names of subjects and their classification numbers or letters (as in Table 23), to direct readers to the parts of the library in which books on different subjects are shelved. On each shelf, books on a particular aspect of a subject — with similar book numbers — are arranged in alphabetical order according to the author, editor, or originator. This helps you to find a particular book quickly, and helps you or a librarian return it to the same place. It follows from this that if any book has been put on the wrong shelf or in the wrong place on a shelf it may not be possible to find it. It is better to leave a book on the table where you have been working, so that it can be shelved by a librarian, than to return it to the wrong place; and in some libraries readers are asked to return all books to an issue desk — even if they have not taken them out of the library.

Current issues of *magazines and journals* are usually kept together, separate from the books, in the reference section of a library, and back numbers are kept in a store to which readers may not have direct access.

No library can afford to buy all the thousands of magazines and journals (periodicals) published each year. Consult the periodicals catalogue (an alphabetical list in your library) to see which periodicals are purchased regularly.

In magazines and journals, original articles and up-to-date reviews are published. Your teachers are in the best position to say which periodicals are likely to be of most use to you, so that you can look regularly at current issues to see if any articles are of interest. Remember also that many journals publish an annual index.

Students who need recent references should, if they need help, tell the librarian what they wish to know and ask for advice on where to find appropriate abstracting or indexing journals. *Abstracts* include only authors' names and the titles and summaries of articles published in selected periodicals. *Indexing journals* include only lists of authors' names and keywords from selected periodicals, which enable you to find articles by particular authors or articles dealing with particular subjects.

Consider *other possible sources of information and ideas*, such as maps and photographs, recorded tapes and slides, videotapes and films. These may be kept in a visual aids section of your library; or they may be available in map rooms or other classrooms.

If the library's catalogues are computer-based, such non-book materials will be included. Also, the librarian will be able to offer advice on open learning and computer-based learning. For example: (a) all the information in a multi-volume encyclopaedia may be available on CD-ROM (Compact Disc Read Only Memory), so called because the user can access (read) but not change this information; and (b) computer-based multimedia (using CD-ROM, video discs, and loudspeakers or headphones) integrate displayed text and diagrams, and photographs, film or video, and sound.

Further information on information retrieval is included in Chapter 11, to help you prepare an extended essay, dissertation, or project report. See also Figure 16.

READ ACCORDING TO YOUR PURPOSE

When you open a book, first look at the date of publication, printed on the reverse of the title page. Look also to see when the book was reprinted or revised. Minor corrections may be made when a book is reprinted but a new edition normally indicates an extensive revision. Always consider how up to date the work is before you read further: you will have to refer to other books, as well or instead, if you require more recent information and ideas.

When you have decided what to read, remember that an effort is required of the reader as well as of the writer. Read carefully to make sure that you take the intended meaning. Read critically as a stimulus to thinking. If possible, obtain information from more than one source. This will help you to see the subject from more than one point of view.

However, remember that what you read is not necessarily true. You may read to get the facts of the matter but the more you read the more you may find that experts disagree. Read critically,

Lost in words

Figure 16 The time spent on the search for information must be carefully related to the time available for the work

therefore: consider the evidence and arguments presented and try to distinguish facts from opinions.

Read with a purpose to see how other people organize and present their thoughts, or to get background information and ideas, or in search of information on specific points. You do not need to read the whole of every book or article that you consult (see Figure 16). Some books are written as reference books but even those that can be read as a whole may also be read in part. Look at the preface to see the author's intentions, and use the contents pages and the index. Get into the habit of skim-reading to find just the information that you need at the time. This is a good way to start reading about a subject, because you will remember best those things that interest you most.

Make notes as you read

Do not waste time copying long passages from your textbooks or making detailed notes. If you do this as a habit, consider whether or not your time could be better spent. Also, remember that if your notes are voluminous they may be too long for use in revision for examinations.

Buy up-to-date textbooks on each aspect of your course and then learn in two ways: by reading the relevant parts of each book several times; and by preparing concise notes.

Unless you intend to read the whole of any book, decide what information you require and then go immediately to relevant pages.

Keep a note of everything you read. Start your notes, as a heading, with complete bibliographic details of the publication. If it is a book, record the author's or editor's name and initials, or the originator's name (see p. 106), the date the book was published (see p. 108), its title (underlined), the edition number, the place of publication, and the name of the publisher.

Example

GASH, S (1989) Effective literature searching for students. Aldershot, Gower.

If you are reading an article in a journal or magazine, note the author's name and initials, the date of publication, the title of the article, the name of the publication (underlined), the volume number, the part number in parenthesis, and the first and last of the page numbers covered by the article.

Example

DeLACEY, G, RECORD, C and WADE, J (1985) How accurate are quotations and references in medical journals? British Medical Journal **291**, (6499) 884–6.

You must be consistent in the way you record such complete bibliographic details, which you will need if you are to consult the same work again or refer someone else to this source of information. In your notes also record: the name of the library from which you obtained the publication, and the shelf or book number; and in the left-hand margin, the number of each page from which you extract ideas or information. This too will save you time if you need to refer to the work again, or refer someone else to a particular page (see p. 113).

All your notes should be concise, but there is no one correct way

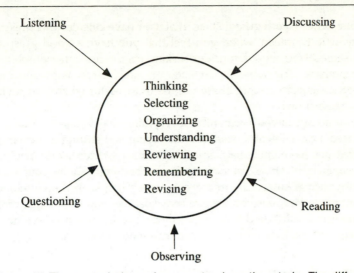

Figure 17 The central place of your notes in active study. The different ways in which making notes contributes to learning are included in the circle. The arrows indicate additions to your notes and to your knowledge and understanding, from different sources

to make notes. You may use different methods on different occasions, depending on your purpose and the way the information is presented for your consideration. The notes you make when planning an essay, to stimulate your own thoughts, may be set out quite differently from those made as you read a book. Then your notes will probably be arranged in order − similar to the author's topic outline − and they may be most useful to you when preparing a topic outline for a composition of your own, to remind you of relevant topics and supporting evidence (see p. 31).

Concise notes are an aid to study. Making notes helps you to concentrate, because you have to decide which paragraphs are relevant to your immediate needs, consider the author's words, make sure you understand, and decide what, if anything, you need to note. It is best to read selected paragraphs carefully and then make concise notes, in your own words, as you read them again. Include numbered headings, use letters (a), (b), etc. for supporting details; use capital letters for important words you wish to remember; use arrows to indicate connections; and use tables and diagrams to summarize information or ideas.

Good, concise notes made as you read are also an aid to revision. It is best if they can be brief notes added to or combined with your lecture notes (see Figure 17), so that you have one set of notes on each subject. Indeed, when you feel that you have a good grasp of any subject you should consider making even more concise notes. If you prepare such *notes of your notes* on index cards, with one card for each subject or topic, these will be most useful when you revise for examinations.

You do not have to remember everything that you write but you do need a convenient system for classifying and storing information so that you have immediate access to all your written work. You can use paperclips to hold A4 sheets together and you can file your work on a particular subject in an A4 envelope. Then keep the envelopes in order in a cardboard box (e.g. a cereal packet); and keep index cards in order in a cardboard box (e.g. a shoe box). More expensive hard-cover files, box files, and filing drawers are not necessary.

IMPROVE YOUR WRITING

Use your notes

When you have to answer a question, do not refer to your notes until you have prepared a first draft of your topic outline (see p. 30). This will help you to produce an original answer. You can then revise your topic outline as you consult your notes or refer to books.

Cite sources of information

In your own compositions do not copy complete sentences from books or other publications and present them as your own (see p. 36). If you extract whole sentences or even paragraphs from any publication, the quotation may be indented (as on pp. 2–3). Note that the author's name, the date of publication, and the title of the work should all be given. It is not necessary to use quotation marks, but every word and punctuation mark must be copied correctly and the title should be underlined (see p. 92).

If a quotation is included as part of a paragraph, without indentation, quotation marks must be used, and the source given. However, in scholarly writing it is more usual to summarize information or ideas from your reading, in your own words, than to quote another person's exact words. Sources of information must still be indicated: (a) to acknowledge the work of others; (b) to indicate to the reader where further relevant information is to be found; and (c) so that, as a student, you can demonstrate to a marker or assessor an awareness of these sources, and your ability to select only relevant publications and integrate information gathered from these publications with that obtained from other sources.

Two methods of citing sources are widely used in scholarly writing. One involves the use of numbers at the end of a statement (in parentheses or superscript). A numbered list of sources is then included at the end of the composition (in the order in which they are first cited). In the other method, which students are advised to use, the name of the originator of a publication (usually the author of a book or paper) is followed by the date on which the book or journal was published. The names of authors are then included, in alphabetical order, below the heading *References* at the end of the composition. The advantages of this name and date method, for students especially, include the following. (a) You will probably remember the names of authors, and the dates of important publications in your subject, but you cannot remember the complete bibliographic details of every work cited. So, in examinations only the name and date method is practicable. (b) In both coursework and examinations you are writing for people who will recognize the names and dates and appreciate their relevance without having to consult your list of references.

When citing a source you may write the author's surname, followed by the year of publication in parenthesis, and then write what the author considers or states. Alternatively, you may include a summary of the author's views, findings, or conclusions, and then end your sentence with the author's surname and the year of publication in parenthesis. For example:

(a) Quiller-Couch (1916) listed words that should be used with care by writers who wish to avoid jargon.
(b) Words that should be used sparingly and with care, by those who wish to avoid jargon, include case, character and nature (Quiller-Couch, 1916).

Either way, you may be asked to include the relevant page number or numbers immediately after the date, particularly if you quote an author's actual words. For example, you could refer to Quiller-Couch (1916: 87) as having listed words to avoid.

If your composition does not end with a list of references, you could write the title of the publication, the date of publication, and the author's name, to indicate a source of information or ideas (as on p. 15).

List references at the end of your compositions

Every coursework assignment you write should end with a list of any works cited in that composition. You should be given credit for having done relevant background reading, as indicated by the sources cited in appropriate parts of your composition; for the understanding made clear in your composition; for your ability to integrate relevant information from different sources; and, if appropriate, for your critical analysis. Start citing sources from the beginning of your course, in your compositions. Do not wait until you have to prepare a longer dissertation or report.

In some subjects, especially arts subjects, it is usual to include a bibliography – not a list of references – at the end of each composition. This may include works consulted in the preparation of your composition, which have influenced your thinking, even if these are not cited in your composition.

In other subjects, especially the sciences and engineering, the preferred heading is *References*. There are two rules. (a) Cite no publication unless you have had it in your hands and read the whole work, or just selected parts, to ensure that you do not misrepresent the author. (b) List complete bibliographic details of every publication cited in your composition, but no others, in alphabetical order according to the authors' names.

You are advised to record complete bibliographic details every time you make notes from a publication, and the number of each page from which you make notes (see p. 110). Examples of complete bibliographic details are given on p. 110 and in Appendix 4: *Further Reading*. Note that the names of publications (the titles of books and the names of journals, for example) are always printed in italics but in your coursework they should be underlined (see p. 92). Do not use quotation marks. For further information on how to cite sources and list references, for example to works by more than one author and to different types of publications, note how these things are done in publications recommended for further reading as part of your course of study. You are also advised to read *Citing and referencing published material* BS 5605 (British Standards Institution, 1990), which provides concise instructions and examples.

Chapter 10

Answering questions in examinations

PREPARING FOR EXAMINATIONS

Only you can decide how you should prepare for examinations, but consider the following suggestions.

Early in your course, obtain a copy of the course programme so that you have a good idea of the course content, and study either the list of learning outcomes included in your course guide or the published syllabus on which your coursework and examination assessments will be based. But remember that your only complete guide to the course content, and so to what may be expected in examinations, should be your own lecture notes, your practical work and other coursework assignments, the lists provided for background reading, and the examination papers set in previous years of the course.

Work steadily throughout your course and keep up to date with all set work. Those who hand in work late create a poor impression of themselves; and those who always hand in work on time are most likely to be in control of their studies.

Make sure that you understand all aspects of your work as you go along, and that you have a good set of notes (see pp. 9 and 109).

Obtain recent question papers so that you can see how the papers are arranged, what choice of questions is given in each subject, and what kinds of questions are asked. Plan answers to the kinds of questions that are likely to be set in your examinations. If you are uncertain of the precise meaning of any question, or exactly what is required in the answer, discuss this with a lecturer. Planning answers will help you to concentrate on your studies and will give direction to your work.

Prepare a timetable for your revision and start this final revision six to eight weeks before your examinations. Remember that in revising you should be simply refreshing your memory. That is to say, you should not be learning things for the first time.

Revise each subject over the whole revision period, not one subject at a time. Work on your notes of your notes (see p. 112) and revise all parts of your work so that it does not matter too much if some of your favourite topics are not examined.

Some people like to work on the evening before an examination. Others find it best to try to put their work on one side and to relax.

Check the date, time and location of each examination. Get enough sleep in the weeks before your examinations and especially on the night before each examination. Make arrangements to ensure that you wake on time.

WHY MANY STUDENTS UNDERACHIEVE IN EXAMINATIONS

The following comments are based on the reports of examiners on advanced school examinations taken by eighteen-year-old students. They apply equally to students in further and higher education.

Use of out-of-date books. Students cannot expect to get a modern approach to their subject from a textbook written many years ago.

Poor allocation of time. Because they do not read the instructions at the head of the examination paper, some candidates answer too few questions, some answer too many, and some do not select questions as directed.

Because they do not discipline themselves to organize their time effectively, many candidates spend too much time on some questions and too little on others — as they run out of time. As a result, they may get good marks for some questions but very few for others, with the result that their final mark is not a true reflection of their ability.

Similarly, candidates lose marks if they do not organize their time effectively within each answer. In most answers it is necessary to exercise judgement in deciding how much time to devote to each part of the answer. But in a structured question the allocation of marks may be given in the margin and this is an indication of how much time should be allocated to each part of the answer.

Lack of care in selecting questions when there is a choice. Candidates must read all questions carefully, to make sure that they understand what is required in each answer, before they decide which questions they can best answer. Otherwise they may find, after leaving the examination room, that they have not made a sensible choice.

Lack of thought before starting an answer. Either because they do not read the question carefully or because they do not think carefully enough about what is required, many candidates write long and painstaking answers but are given very few marks — simply because they include much irrelevant material and do not do precisely what is asked of them.

The candidates who think, select relevant material, and plan concise answers to the questions set will score many more marks than those who write at greater length — who reproduce copious notes or are determined to write *all they know* about the subject in the hope that the examiner will look for anything that happens to be relevant and delete everything that is irrelevant. In practice, examiners do not waste their time on doing things that the candidates should do for themselves. Quality, completeness, and relevance are required — not quantity for its own sake.

Answering a similar question, perhaps one set in a previous year, instead of the question set. Many candidates, having carefully prepared an answer before entering the examination room — as part of their revision — seem to be incapable of readjusting. They are not prepared to reorganize their knowledge of the subject so that they can present a considered answer to the question set.

Giving an incomplete answer. Some candidates do not answer part of the question because they either do not plan their answer or do not work to their topic outline.

Other candidates obviously have planned their answer but they omit evidence or examples, or omit other relevant material — perhaps because they think it is too elementary. It is best to include all relevant aspects of an answer to the question asked, even if some introductory material is mentioned only briefly and in passing. Otherwise, the examiner must assume that you are ignorant of some parts of the answer.

Failure to make clear one's understanding of the material presented. Marks are given not simply for relevant material, well ordered and clearly presented, but also for understanding.

Candidates must show they understand why all parts of an

answer are relevant to the question set. For example, words from the question may be used at appropriate points in the answer to draw attention to the relevance of what is being presented.

Poor presentation. Candidates should consider the examiner, who has many papers to mark, and should take a pride in the way they present their work (see p. 40). They should start by indicating clearly the number of the question being answered; and should make sure that their writing is legible. A careless scrawl makes an unfavourable impression from the start — and examiners can give marks only for what they can read.

Candidates should not leave gaps, for example at the bottom of a page, and then continue the answer on a later page. Otherwise the examiner may give a mark and then find, on turning the page, that the answer is continued and that the mark already given must be reconsidered.

Inadequate vocabulary. Many candidates are frustrated because they cannot find the words to express their thoughts precisely and completely.

In scholarly writing try to avoid clichés, colloquial expressions and slang, which are all signs of an inadequate vocabulary.

Poor spelling. Spelling words incorrectly always creates an unfavourable impression, and it can result in misunderstandings.

Poor punctuation and grammar. Some candidates do not understand even the simpler rules of punctuation. Because of errors in punctuation and grammar such candidates write ambiguous sentences. But examiners can mark only what is written — not what they think the candidate probably meant.

IMPROVE YOUR EXAMINATION TECHNIQUE

Most of the faults listed on pp. 116–18 can be summed up in three words: poor examination technique.

The following advice can be understood by a student working alone, but may also be used by teachers in class discussions both before and after a test or examination.

If possible, examination scripts should be returned to students so that they can see their mistakes and appreciate where they have failed to express themselves clearly.

Consider how examination papers are set and marked

Consider how examination papers are marked so that in planning each answer you can try to score maximum marks. Learn to see each part of any answer, and each paragraph, as an opportunity to gain marks by adding *relevant* information and ideas, and by showing your understanding.

1 In most examinations marks are divided equally between the questions to be answered so that there are 25 marks per question when four questions are to be answered, and 20 marks per question when five are to be answered. You must, therefore, answer the right number of questions.

2 To be fair to all candidates, examiners allocate the marks which may be obtained for each question according to a marking scheme. This is a topic outline, similar to the one that you will prepare before you start your answer.

If a question is set in parts, a certain number of marks will be allocated for each part of the answer. However, whether or not the question is set in parts, the examiner will expect you to refer to, and to show your understanding of, all those things which are relevant to the answer.

If you do not answer all parts of a question or if you give an answer that is otherwise incomplete, you cannot score full marks on that question.

Make good use of your time in examinations

1 Read and obey all the instructions at the top of the first page of the question paper. Make sure that you know how much time you are allowed and how many questions you must answer. Look to see if there are any compulsory questions, or any restrictions on your choice of questions.

2 If you have a choice of questions read them all carefully to make sure that you understand what is required in each answer. Then select the questions that you can answer most fully. Otherwise you may realize, after leaving the examination, that you could have answered another selection of questions and obtained better marks.

3 Allocate your time so that you can answer the right number of questions. The instructions at the head of the paper may give guidance about how much time you should spend on the parts of

a paper. If the number of marks allocated to a question (or to the parts of a question) is stated in the right-hand margin of the question paper or at the end of the question, this should help you to allocate your time.

If all questions carry the same number of marks, divide your time equally between the questions. Do not spend more time on those questions that you know most about. Remember that it is easier to score half marks on a question that you do not know much about than it is to score full marks when you think you can write a good answer. The first few marks are the easiest to obtain, with a little thought, if you know anything about the subject. But a little extra time spent on a question, upon which you have already spent long enough, is likely to be less rewarding.

4 Keep an eye on the time. Allow a proportion of the time available for reading all the questions at the beginning, for planning your answers, and for reading through your work at the end to correct any slips of the pen and to add any important points that you did not remember the first time through.

5 If in spite of planning you find that you are running out of time, it is better to answer your last question in note form than to leave it unanswered. In a written examination you will be given some marks for a good topic outline.

6 Do not waste time. Arrive at the examination before the start but try to relax: do not talk to others about the examination while you are waiting to enter the room. Use your time effectively during the examination. Do not leave before the end.

How to answer questions in examinations

An examination is a test not only of your knowledge of the subject but also of your ability to understand the questions and to organize your knowledge in effective answers.

1 Read the question carefully to make sure that you understand what the examiner wants to know. Answer the question that you have been asked and *not a similar question which you were hoping for.*

2 If the examination comprises essay-type questions, you may find it best to plan all your answers quickly at the beginning of the examination — so that you can reconsider each topic

outline immediately before you start to write each answer.
3 Mark the number of the question clearly in the left-hand margin of your answer book at the start of your answer. Do not waste time copying out the question.
4 In an examination you cannot spend much time on thinking about how to begin. However, in your first paragraph you will probably use some words or phrases from the question in a context that makes clear to the examiner that you do understand the question. Indeed, the first sentence or paragraph, if appropriate, should give the essence of your answer.
5 Get to the point quickly and keep to the point. Plan your answer so that it is well organized and well balanced, and so that you can say all that you wish to say without digression or repetition in the time available. By distinct paragraph breaks and, if appropriate, by concise subheadings, make clear to the examiner where one aspect of the question has been dealt with and the next begins.
6 Do not make vague statements. Give reasons and examples. Include enough explanation. Do not leave things out because you think they are too simple or too obvious. Do not include anything that is irrelevant but make sure that everything relevant is included, however briefly, to show your knowledge and understanding. Your answer must be complete, because the examiner cannot assume that you know anything, and can give marks only for what you write.
7 If you include anything that is not obviously relevant, explain why it is relevant. An examination is not simply a test of your ability to recall facts and ideas. It also provides an opportunity to show your ability to distinguish relevant from irrelevant material.
8 If you are asked to discuss then you must discuss all sides of the question and refer to any unsolved problems.
9 If you are asked to compare you should also refer to any differences, even if the question does not ask you to compare and contrast. If you are asked to compare two things, do not simply describe one and then the other. In every paragraph, after the introduction, make comparisons and point out differences.
10 If a question is set in several parts it is best to answer each part separately, and if the parts are indicated by letters (a, b, c, etc.) you should use these letters to indicate the parts of your

Do not waste time on shading

Figure 18 In an examination use all your time effectively

answer. If the parts of a question are not labelled by letters, you should use appropriate subheadings to draw attention to the parts of your answer that relate to each part of the question.

11 If a question is set in several parts, you must spend enough time on each part of your answer. Unless you have some very good reason for not doing so, you should answer the parts in the order in which they are set, because the examiner will expect to mark them in this order.

12 If the number of marks allocated to each part of a question is indicated in the margin (next to the question), this should indicate not only how much time you should devote to each part of your answer but also how many relevant points may be needed for an adequate answer to each part.

13 Make sure that any diagram is simple so that you can complete it quickly and neatly. Use coloured pencils, if necessary, to represent different things, but do not waste time on shading (see Figure 18).

Each diagram should be in the most appropriate place but should be numbered so that you can refer to it in other parts of your answer. If diagrams are necessary they should complement your writing – making explanation easier and enabling you to present information and ideas that could not be adequately presented in words alone. Effective diagrams should therefore reduce the number of words needed in the text. Do not waste time conveying the same information both in words and in a diagram.

14 In an examination you will not be able to remember complete bibliographic details of publications, so you will not be expected to end each composition with a Bibliography or List of References cited. However, you can cite sources, using the name and date system, and you are advised to do so (for reasons, see pp. 112–13).

15 Make sure that your writing is legible and use black or blue-black ink. Do not write with a coloured pen or pencil.

16 Put a sloping line through any rough work; and to make a correction put a sloping line through any letter or a horizontal line through any word you need to delete. Then make a correction in the space between your lines of writing.

How to answer questions in tests

In many courses students are assessed on their coursework as well as, or instead of, in examinations. The coursework includes different kinds of assignments, assessed by the quality of written compositions (see Chapters 4 and 11), and may also include tests that have to be completed in a limited time under examination conditions.

In addition to contributing to assessment, regular tests enable lecturers to recognize misconceptions or misunderstandings shared by many students, so that these can be corrected, and to identify particular students who need extra tuition or counselling.

Most tests set as part of coursework comprise questions that require only short answers. As a result: (a) questions may be set on all aspects of the course; (b) the student may be required to answer all the questions; and (c) the question-answering technique required is quite different from that required in the kind of examinations considered on pp. 119–23:

1 Read and obey all the instructions at the top of the first page of the question paper. This is important in all tests and examinations but is especially important if the paper is to be scanned by an

optical mark reader and the data analysed by a computer.

2 If you have to answer all the questions, it is a waste of time to read them all before you start to write.

3 The number of marks allocated to each question should be clearly stated. This (a) gives you an idea as to how much of the time available for the whole test should be devoted to answering the question, and (b) may help you to decide how many different points are expected in your answer.

4 There may be space, after each question, for you to write your answer on the question paper. If there is, this indicates the length of answer expected. Do not write more.

5 Read the first question. Think about it. What exactly is required? If you know the answer, consider how it can be clearly expressed. Think and plan, however briefly, then write your answer.

6 Answer the questions, in order, thinking carefully before you write.

7 If the answer to a question does not immediately come to mind, or if you think at first reading that you do not know the answer, do not waste time at this stage just sitting and thinking, or worrying. Put a question mark in the margin, to remind you to reconsider this question later, if you have time, and proceed to the next question.

8 When you have worked through the question paper once, making sure you answer all the questions you find easy, look again at each of the questions you have not yet answered. You may now realize just what is required, or remember the answer.

9 If you are not sure of the answer to any question, and if no marks are deducted for an incorrect answer, you have nothing to lose by guessing. If you know something about the subject, a considered answer is more likely to be right than wrong. And you cannot score marks for any question, or any part of a question, if you make no attempt at an answer.

10 Never leave a test before the end. Read all the questions again, if you have time. Check that you have answered the question set, and that your answer is clearly expressed.

IMPROVE YOUR WRITING

Revise regularly

Work to a timetable throughout your course of study and revise all aspects of your work regularly. For example, at the weekend you may review aspects of the previous week's work, and in vacations you should revise the previous term's or year's work as well as looking forward to the term or year ahead. It is not possible to revise everything in the few weeks preceding an examination unless you have understood, learned, and revised throughout the course.

Develop your interest

Try not only to keep abreast of your work but also to master your subject. Teachers find that they learn most when they have to teach their subject. In preparing topic outlines it may help if you think about what you would say if you had to teach this aspect of your subject, and if you consider the kinds of questions that your students might ask.

Also, to maintain and develop your interest in the course, consider your studies in a wider perspective. For example, try to obtain relevant vacation employment.

Study past examination papers

List the questions set on each topic in recent examinations (for example, in the past two years). Incorporate these lists in the relevant parts of your notes, followed by the topic outlines prepared as you study and revise.

Practise answering examination questions

To develop your ability to work under pressure, as in examinations, test yourself regularly by writing answers to questions in the time that will be allowed in an examination. Also, complete some past papers to give yourself practice in finishing the number of questions required in the set time.

Always write on wide-lined paper, which is the kind that is provided in most examinations, and leave a 25 mm margin on the left-hand side of each page.

Chapter 11

Writing a dissertation, extended essay, term paper or project report

In advanced courses especially, students may have the opportunity to work independently on an aspect of their subject that is of particular interest to them, but with a supervisor to advise and help when necessary. The composition prepared as a result of this special study may be called a *dissertation*: a setting forth of the results of a study of documents, or a review of relevant published work, or both, and including argument, evidence, explanation, and perhaps also description, and leading to some conclusion. Such a study may also be called an *extended essay*, which simply means it is longer than the answers to questions submitted for assessment in other course-work; or it may be called a *term paper*, which indicates that more time is allowed for this work than is needed for preparing most coursework assignments.

A *project report* is considered here to be similar to a dissertation but differing in that it is based on personal observations or surveys, involving the collection of qualitative and quantitative data, the analysis of these original data, the interpretation of the results of this analysis, and a consideration of these results in relation to relevant published work.

Preparing a longer composition is a test of a student's ability (a) to demonstrate knowledge, understanding and critical evaluation of relevant documents or publications; (b) to communicate information and ideas in writing, supported, if appropriate, by tables and diagrams; and (c) to complete the work in a given time. The advice included in earlier chapters should be considered as well as the further advice in this chapter.

Projects are assessed not weighed

Figure 19 Do not attempt too much

AGREE YOUR TERMS OF REFERENCE WITH YOUR SUPERVISOR

Your supervisor will help you to define the purpose and scope of your special study so that you know exactly what is required, and will try to ensure you can complete the task in the time available (see Figure 19) without neglecting your other studies or interfering with your preparation for examinations.

Before starting, make sure any essential equipment, documents, or other materials will be available when you need them. Check that any essential publications are available in your library or can be obtained from elsewhere when you need them.

Choose a subject in which you are already interested and which will complement and support your other studies. If possible, look at satisfactory reports completed by other students in previous years of your course to get an idea of what they were able to do in the time available to you. Do not attempt too much.

In other coursework, and in examinations, you have to prepare written answers to questions. Each question must be carefully worded so that you know exactly what is required in your answer. Similarly, in business or industry any report is preceded by clearly worded *terms of reference*. These state the purpose of the work and its scope. Your extended essay or project report will have a concise title, and this should either be in itself, or be followed by, a clear statement of your terms of reference.

FIND OUT HOW YOUR WORK WILL BE ASSESSED

An extended essay or project may provide an opportunity for you to display initiative, ingenuity, and originality; and an opportunity for you to demonstrate your ability to select relevant material and present this in a way that is appropriate for the intended audience. Your extended essay or project report should therefore indicate, as appropriate, not only what you have done but also your approach to the problems involved, to the interpretation of work done by others, and to the analysis and interpretation of any new observations. Because of all these things, as in all other coursework, what you write and how you write will play a major part in the assessment of your work.

It is difficult for an examiner to arrive at an objective assessment of project work. This is particularly true for an external examiner who has not been in any way associated with the work. Unless there is an oral examination, the extended essay or project report is the external examiner's only guide to the quality of the work.

It may be difficult for any examiner to decide how much of the report is the student's own work and how much is the supervisor's. All students need help in limiting the scope of their special study, but once this has been agreed the supervisor should provide clear terms of reference in writing so that there is no possibility of misunderstandings later. The supervisor should also try to ensure that the work begins well.

Some dissertations and project reports provide more opportunities than others for students to show initiative, ingenuity, and originality; and different students have different supervisors. These differences, which make objective assessment difficult, must be considered carefully if all students are to be treated fairly.

There is probably no one correct solution to these problems but it is possible to list criteria that should influence the final assessment. These cannot all be judged at the end of the work.

1 The student's ability to define clearly the problem to be tackled or the purpose of the work, if the subject was chosen by the student.

2 The thoroughness with which the work was tackled in relation to the time available, and the planning of the work.
3 The accuracy with which information is recorded.
4 The student's ability to evaluate published work, to make original observations, to record and analyse data (as appropriate), to argue logically, and to draw valid conclusions.
5 The student's ability to relate personal observations and findings to the published work of others.
6 The student's ability to select relevant material and reject what is irrelevant. A good student will write a clear, concise, considered, critical, balanced, well-organized, and well-presented dissertation or report. In contrast, an incomplete, opinionated, superficial, or uncritical composition, with inadequate reference to relevant sources, will be recognized as lacking rigour.

These aspects of the work might be considered of comparable importance and given equal weight in a marking scheme. But whatever method of assessment is adopted, each student needs to know, before the work is started, how the extended essay or project report is to be presented and how the work as a whole will be assessed.

Different kinds of work will be reported in different ways, and notes for guidance will normally be issued to students taking a particular course. For example, see p. 142.

DECIDE ON EFFECTIVE HEADINGS

A dissertation based on a literature search and reading, with no supporting personal observations, will be written as an extended essay or review. As in any other essay, you will include an introduction and a conclusion but the body of the essay will comprise many paragraphs. These must be arranged in an effective order, and you will help yourself and your readers if you group closely related paragraphs below appropriate headings and subheadings. You must therefore plan your work just as you would plan any other composition.

In a project involving the collection and analysis of data, as well as the study of relevant published work, the project report may be arranged as in Table 24.

Using the accepted headings, and knowing the kind of information placed by convention below each heading, makes writing easier and

Table 24 The parts of a project report

Part	Content
Cover sheet	Full title of project. Your name. Name of course of study of which the project is part. Name of institution. Date.
Title page	Full title of project. Your name.
Acknowledgements	Who helped?
List of contents	Headings and main subheadings used in report.
Introduction	Why did you do the work? What was the problem? If a literature survey is required, include a subheading as part of your introduction.
Methods	How did you do it?
Results	What did you find?
Discussion	What do you make of your results? How do they compare with those of others?
Conclusions	What do you conclude? Are you able to answer any of the questions raised in your *Introduction*?
Summary	What are your main findings?
Sources of information	Give full bibliographic details (see p. 110) for every publication cited in your report but no others.
Appendices	Include, for example, tables of data collected in your investigations and summarized in your *Results*.

helps readers to find answers to their questions: What? Why? When? How? Where? Who?

Another type of project, preparing an instruction manual, may be appropriate in some courses. See the advice on preparing instructions (Chapter 3). The project report may then be arranged as follows: Cover; Title page; Acknowledgements; List of contents; Description of equipment; Operating instructions; Maintenance instructions; Servicing instructions; Fault-finding and fault correction. In a technical report it is usual to number section headings (1, 2, 3, etc.) and subheadings (1.1, 1.2, 1.3, etc.), and if necessary the paragraphs under each subheading (1.1.1, 1.1.2, 1.1.3, etc.). This helps the writer ensure that all sections and paragraphs are in order, and it facilitates precise cross-referencing (to sections, subsections, or paragraphs rather than to pages).

In other courses, a suitable project might be the preparation of a guide to the organization and work of an agency, institution, firm, or service. Such a project report might be arranged as follows: Cover; Title page; Acknowledgements; List of contents; Introduction (including the reasons for the existence of the agency, institution, etc., and the purpose of the project report); Method of inquiry (including how the information presented in the report was obtained, and what problems were encountered); Results (of the inquiry); Conclusions; Summary; Sources of information; Appendices.

Whatever the nature of your dissertation or project, you will work on it for many weeks and your written account will probably be longer and more demanding than anything you have written previously. It must be carefully planned so that each aspect of your work can be reported in the most appropriate place. Consider the suggestions on arrangement made in this chapter, but do not be bound by conventions if you have some good reason for preferring a different arrangement or different headings.

Decide how to arrange your essay or report after you have discussed your ideas with your supervisor and have read the relevant parts of any syllabus, regulations, or notes for guidance provided by your supervisor or published by the examiners. You must follow any instructions included in these regulations or notes for guidance. They are intended to help you with your writing, to encourage uniformity in presentation, to make for easy reading, and so to facilitate assessment.

WRITE FROM THE START

Do not complete your investigations or literature search and then start to write, and do not spend so much time on these things that you have no time to write (see Figure 16). On the contrary, as soon as you have agreed on the title and scope of the work with your supervisor, try to allocate your time to thinking and planning, to the search for information or to collecting and analysing data, and to writing and revising (see Figure 20). Remember that you will need time for preparing diagrams. If the report is to be typed you must also leave time for this even if you do not do the typing yourself.

When you are writing an extended essay or project report,

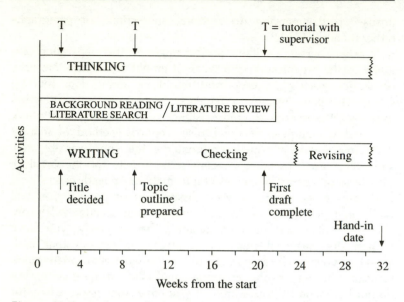

Figure 20 Preparing a dissertation: allocating your time to different activities

imagine that you are writing not only for your supervisor but also for an external examiner, whose precise interests you will not know. If you are preparing an instruction manual, make sure that it can be understood by the kind of person who is most likely to use the equipment. Whatever you are writing, first try to identify your readers and then keep their needs in mind.

When working on any long composition, if you are not using a word processor you are advised to keep carbon copies of everything you write – in a different place from your top copies. If you do not do this, and you lose your only copy, you will have to start work on your composition again – from the beginning. At best this will interfere with your other studies; at worst you may not have time to complete your composition.

Start writing as soon as you have decided what to study. Writing a first draft of the Introduction will concentrate your attention on the purpose of your composition and its relationship to other people's work. This should help you to see your limited objective, clearly stated in your terms of reference, in a wider perspective.

In a project report, in science, the Introduction must include a clear statement of the *problem* investigated – which may be stated as a question. If an experiment is reported, the *hypothesis* tested — a possible answer to the question — should also be stated.

In a dissertation or extended essay, in any subject, the Introduction may include a *proposition*: a statement offered for consideration, which will be followed in the rest of the composition by argument, supported by evidence, and which in the last paragraph you may conclude is probably correct, or you may reject, or for which you may have insufficient evidence to reach either conclusion. Or your Introduction may include your *thesis*: a proposition which you state clearly and which in the rest of your composition you seek to maintain — again by argument and supporting evidence.

To *argue* in this context does not mean to disagree, but to present a case supported by evidence. You may present evidence for and then evidence against, or vice versa, depending on your conclusion, or you may present weak points in your argument first and the strongest last, leading to your conclusion; or you may present the views of others first and your own last — as your conclusion. Your argument is the thread that runs through the whole composition, and the *evidence* presented may include recorded observations (data), and the results of the analysis of data. Starting from a true *premise* (a proposition which until proved otherwise is accepted as a fact), *logical argument* should lead to a valid conclusion. The word *valid* may refer to a reason, an objection, or as here to a conclusion: it simply means that the reason, objection, or conclusion is well founded.

In a project report, write the Methods section as soon as you have decided how you will do the work. And then write an account of each part of your investigation, for the Results section, as soon as it is complete — so that, if necessary, you can easily check your work. Throughout the work, make notes of points you may include in your Discussion as they come to mind. Then, when the work is complete, you can write the Discussion section of your report and revise all other sections.

Prepare tables and illustrations to be included in the Methods, Results or Discussion sections of a project report, or in any part of a dissertation, as your work proceeds. There should be only one table or illustration on any page, unless you wish to facilitate comparison. Each table or illustration should, if possible, fit upright on the page and diagrams that are to be compared must be drawn to the same scale.

SEARCH THE LITERATURE

In a dissertation the whole work may be a critical literature review; and in a project report, in addition to citing relevant published work in the Introduction, Methods and Discussion sections, the subheading *Literature review* may be required as part of the Introduction. Whether you are preparing an extended essay, dissertation, or project report, finding relevant publications is a time-consuming but essential part of your work. Completing a literature review enables you to:

1 decide on the scope of your composition;
2 write about your own findings in the context of previous work, including recent work;
3 recognize gaps, inconsistencies, different interpretations of evidence, differences of opinion;
4 comment upon and discuss the work of others, and establish the originality of your own work; and
5 add to what is already known.

In undertaking a literature review, start with your supervisor's suggestions and any references provided. Make use of publications available in your own library and in other convenient libraries, including encyclopaedias, handbooks, directories, books, and journals (see Chapter 9).

In some subjects most of the information you require may be available in books, including introductory textbooks, advanced treatises, and research monographs. In other subjects you may find little useful information in books. One reason for this is that publishers may find it uneconomic to produce books for specialists — because few people are likely to buy them. Another reason is that it takes some time to produce a book and authors must complete their literature surveys a year or more before the publication date.

The more specialized your work, or the more recent the published work you need to read, therefore, the less you will be able to rely on books and the more you will need to look at journals that publish the original work of specialists (see p. 107). For the most recent published papers, because your own library can subscribe to only a few of the thousands of journals published each year, you will need to search relevant abstracting and indexing journals (see p. 107). However, you should be aware of relevant review publications in your subject. Some of these are journals, but publish only review articles – each one being a review of the literature on a specialized aspect of a subject. Others are books, with each chapter a review article.

Also, useful information on topics of current interest may be included in conference proceedings (in which each chapter is a paper read at a conference), and in official reports published, for example, by governments and international organizations (each of which will conclude with recommendations).

In addition to leaflets on how to use their catalogues, most academic libraries provide concise guides to the literature on different subjects, and you should ask for the guide to the subject or subjects in which you are interested.

To find books relevant to your dissertation or project, use the catalogues of your own library and those of other convenient libraries (see p. 105). And to find whether a book is in print, consult a list of books in print for example, *Whitaker's Books in Print* or *Books in Print* (see p. 105). For older books consult other bibliographies: some are the published catalogues of major libraries; others are lists of books on specialist subjects.

To find relevant articles in journals you may scan the contents pages of selected journals in your library (for the most recent work), or look at current-awareness publications, which include only the contents pages of major journals in selected subjects (for example, *Current Contents*).

When searching indexing or abstracting journals (see p. 108) you must work to a list of keywords or search terms. These must be selected carefully so that they help you to find only relevant publications. Keep a note of the search terms you are using, and of the issues of the journals you have searched and their location, so that if any are unavailable you can come back to them later, and so that you can add to your list as more are published. Start with the most recent issue. If you find a paper that is of interest to you, it will include a list of references cited and one of these may be an important review article.

In most university libraries and major public libraries, it is possible to enter search terms using a computer terminal connected via national and international telephone and telecommunications networks to bibliographic databases on every subject. Advantages of such computer-based information retrieval include the following:

1 Many years' issues of an abstracting journal can be searched in a few minutes.
2 It is possible to access more sources of information (databases), some of which are available only online.
3 It is possible to search for any word in title, abstract, and description fields.
4 A printout of complete bibliographic details can be produced as the search is performed, and a printed copy of selected references can be ordered.
5 The search can be interactive: you can alter it as it proceeds, in response to the results obtained.
6 Arrangements can be made for a satisfactory search to be repeated each time the database is updated, and for bibliographic details of any new references to be sent to the user.

Disadvantages of online searching include the following:

1 Indexing of the database record may be inconsistent.
2 It may be possible to search only recent years.
3 The databases may be biased towards the publications of one country.
4 Students may not have access to a computer terminal from which an online search can be made, and so may have to rely on a skilled and well-briefed intermediary. The intermediary may ask for (a) the title or terms of reference for your composition, (b) the search terms (keywords) to be used, and related terms or synonyms, (c) details of the sources already searched manually, (d) a key reference if you have one, (e) an indication of the types of document likely to be of interest, (f) the dates to be covered, and (g) the date by which the results of the search are required.

It is not possible to say that an online search is better than a manual search. The online search will include more publications and a printout of many references is likely to be obtained; but other references will be found as a result of a manual search. If there is time, and if it is possible, it is best to use both methods: manual for the library resources available to you, and online for those that otherwise would be inaccessible.

However you work, in a thorough search you are likely to find references to many more publications than you have time to read. On a separate A6 index card (148 × 105 mm), or at the top of a sheet of A4 paper on which, later, you expect to make notes, record complete bibliographic details of each reference (see p. 110), the source of the reference (publication, volume number, and page number), and the location of this source (the name of the library and the book or shelf number). If you request a copy of the publication, on inter-library loan, record also the date of this request.

Try to reduce your list of references to manageable proportions. For some, you may decide from the title that they are not likely to be useful. For each of the others you must decide – from the author's name, the title of the publication, a published abstract, or a reference in a review article – that it is (a) likely to be of immediate interest, or (b) unlikely to be a key work, or (c) unlikely to be relevant to your present needs. You may then be in a position to decide, perhaps after a further discussion with your supervisor, which publications that are not available locally you should try to obtain on inter-library loan.

Inter-library loans are expensive, so you may be limited in the number you can obtain, if any, free of charge. So you will probably send for only those few that you feel are essential for the satisfactory completion of your work, and may have to rely mainly on the resources of local libraries or those you are able to visit when on vacation.

When you have a publication in your hands you should check the bibliographic details and ensure that your record is complete and correct, as there may be mistakes in indices, abstracts, and other publications from which you copied the reference. Then evaluate the publication by reading the abstract, the introduction, and the conclusions, and by studying any tables or figures. If it is of interest you can scan the section headings, and decide: (a) how much of it you must study – one page, one part, or the whole work; or (b) that it is not essential reading but may be of interest after you have completed more urgent tasks.

If you use A4 paper for your notes, you may file any photocopies with your notes. But do not allow making a photocopy to become an alternative to reading an important publication critically, as soon as is convenient after you receive it, and making your own notes.

For a student preparing a dissertation or project report there is probably no advantage in entering references on a computer database, unless there is some exceptional reason for doing so. It is easy to cope with the limited number of references likely to be involved by keeping your records in alphabetical order by author on A6 index cards, or on A4 paper (see p. 139), and these have the advantage of being portable – enabling you to enter bibliographic details as you undertake a search, or add notes, or to interleave photocopies in appropriate places in your notes, as you are working in different libraries, in your study, or elsewhere.

REVIEW THE LITERATURE

Sources must be cited to support any reference to published evidence, but if you read critically throughout your course you will find many instances in which experts disagree about the interpretation of evidence, especially if there is conflicting evidence. This is why students may be encouraged to develop a healthy scepticism and to be prepared to question everything. Do not accept published statements or conclusions as being true or correct just because the author is an acknowledged authority. Always consider the evidence presented in relation to other evidence and your own experience. Read critically, and with an enquiring mind. Is this true? What is the evidence? Is it relevant? What are the implications? The results of such critical thinking will be apparent in your writing.

You will recognize *opinions* (views held on the basis of evidence and experience but which are not necessarily correct), *assumptions* (things assumed to be true but which may not be), *assertions* (things stated as if they were true but for which evidence is not provided by the writer), *facts* (things that on the basis of all the evidence at present available are generally accepted as true statements), and *speculation* (which may or may not be well founded, and so could be helpful or misleading). You will draw attention to conflicting statements, to *issues* (points of disagreement), and to *opinions* that seem to be based on insufficient evidence or on preconceived ideas. And you may make comparisons, recognize connections, suggest original *interpretations*, and come to your own conclusions, or point out the need for further research.

There may be times, as you read and accumulate notes, when you feel bogged down in the conflicting interpretations of evidence, and find it impossible to refer to all the available sources of information or cope with the wealth of detail (see Figure 16). Do not be discouraged by this; but do be selective in your search for information. In your reading you will come across many side-issues that you find interesting and may like to return to when you have time. But do not digress: keep your title and your terms of reference in mind and concentrate on material relevant to your immediate needs.

Be prepared to change your mind as you learn more and achieve a deeper understanding. Part of the pleasure to be gained from reading and writing is due not only to increasing knowledge and understanding of the subject itself but also to the enlightenment that comes from enlarging your view of the world, and to the satisfying experience of shaping and presenting your thoughts for later consideration yourself and for consideration by others.

IMPROVE YOUR WRITING

Work on your first draft

To make your work easier, write on one side only of each sheet of paper. Write each heading, each subheading, and even each paragraph on a separate sheet; and prepare each table and illustration on a separate sheet. This will help you (a) to ensure that each paragraph deals with only one topic, (b) to keep information on each aspect of the work together in one place, (c) to avoid repetition, (d) to incorporate new material or change the order of presentation, (e) to remove unwanted material, and (f) to rewrite paragraphs when necessary without having to rewrite the whole composition. In this way, as when using a word processor, while you are working on the draft of your composition it remains an up-to-date progress report. Alternatively, if you intend to word-process your composition, you may prefer to work on a word processor from the start (see Appendix 1).

If you have kept notes, as suggested on p. 109, you will have recorded complete bibliographic details of each source cited in your composition — at the top of a separate page of your notes (or on an index card). When your work is otherwise complete, these can be removed from your file and the details listed in alphabetical order after the heading *Bibliography* or *References*, as appropriate (see p. 114). Remember to list only publications you have studied as part of your work and cited in your composition. Your assessors should be impressed by the thoroughness of your search and your ability to select and evaluate relevant sources, not by the length of your list.

You will probably have revised or rewritten your Introduction several times, and you should check it again when your composition is otherwise complete. Try to ensure that the reader is interested and favourably impressed at the start. The last thing you will write is the summary (at the end) or the abstract (at the beginning). The reader may well read this before the Introduction, so you must devote enough thought to it.

A summary, if one is required, will be at the end of your composition (see Table 24, p. 130) so the reader will also be able to refer to other parts of your composition. But you may be required to provide an abstract, instead of a summary, and this may be placed immediately after the title. If an extra copy of the abstract is required, this will probably be for the external examiner – who may see it first without the rest of your composition. The difference between a summary and an abstract, therefore, is that an abstract may have to stand alone – representing your work in the absence of the composition as a whole (just as when you read an abstract in an abstracting journal).

Check your composition

You cannot check the completed composition properly by reading it through once or twice. It is necessary to check one thing at a time.

1 Are the cover and title pages complete? Do they provide all the information required by your assessors? For example, see Table 24.

2 Does the title provide the best concise description of the contents of your composition?

3 Do you need a contents page? If so, make sure the headings and subheadings are in order and identical with those used in the text.

4 Does each part of the composition start with a main heading at the top of a page?

5 Are the purpose and scope of your composition (or your terms of reference) stated clearly and concisely in the Introduction? Is everything included in the report relevant to the title? Do you keep within the scope of the work as stated in your Introduction; and do you comply with your terms of reference?

6 Has anything essential been left out? Are all your readers' questions answered (see p. 130)? Are your conclusions clearly expressed?

7 Is each paragraph necessary? Is it in the best place? Is the connection between paragraphs clear?

8 Is the composition well balanced? Have you given too much attention to details and neglected essential points? Is there any important point that could be more clearly expressed? Is anything original emphasized sufficiently (see *Emphasis*, p. 91)?

9 Is each statement accurate, based on sufficient evidence, free from contradictions, and free from errors of omission? Are there any words, such as many or few, that should be replaced by numbers?

10 Are there any mistakes in spelling or grammar?

11 Could the meaning of any sentence be better expressed? Is each sentence easy to read? Does it sound well when read aloud?

12 Are any technical terms, symbols, or abbreviations sufficiently explained, and used consistently and correctly?

13 Are all sources cited correctly? If your notes for guidance do not include clear instructions, ask your supervisor for advice on the method of citation to be used (see p. 113).

14 Are all the sources cited in your composition listed correctly at the end, and in alphabetical order? See p. 114 for the difference between a bibliography and a list of references.

15 Are all figures, tables, and pages numbered and in order?

16 Have you referred to each figure and each table at least once in the text? Is any information presented in a table and repeated in a diagram? Do the tables and diagrams support the text, without unnecessary repetition?

17 Does the composition look neat and does it sound well when read aloud?

18 Have you obeyed all instructions provided in the notes for guidance? See p. 129.

When you have completed, checked, and corrected your first draft, your supervisor may like to read it and make suggestions for its improvement. Otherwise, ask someone else to read your work. Readers may be able to point out inconsistencies or mistakes, sentences and paragraphs that are not relevant or are out of place, and parts that are ambiguous or difficult to understand. Consider these comments and then make any necessary additions, deletions, or corrections. You may need to rewrite your composition before you hand it in for assessment.

Typing instructions

If you are to have your composition typed, you must ensure that it is legible and is neatly laid out for the typist — and that any instructions about arrangement and presentation are clearly stated. These may be included in the notes for guidance provided by your supervisor, or in the course assessment regulations, or in your course guide. If they are, the typist will need a copy of these notes. If they are not, the typist will require instructions from you, such as the following.

1 Use A4 paper.
2 Leave a 40 mm margin on the left and 25 mm margin on the right, top, and bottom of each page.
3 Use a standard typeface (not italics) and type in double spacing on only one side of each sheet.
4 Start each main heading at the top of a new page. Centre main headings but not side headings.
5 Type each table on a separate sheet.
6 Include separate cover and title pages; and a list of contents.
7 When the tables and figures have been inserted, number all pages (except the cover, title and contents pages) with arabic numerals, at the top right-hand corner.
8 Keep a copy.

Before handing your manuscript to a typist, check that you have used capital letters or underlined words only where you require them, and that the whole composition is set out according to your requirements.

If you type the work yourself, using a typewriter (or a word processor — see Appendix 1), and have not been taught to type, your typing will look better if you leave at least two spaces between words in capital letters, one space between a person's initials, one space after a comma, two after a semicolon or colon, three after a full stop, and five at the start of each new paragraph — except the first after a heading, which should not be indented. If you do not indent at the start of each new paragraph, leave more space between paragraphs than you leave between the lines of type within each paragraph. Remember that you must leave a space between a number and a symbol for an SI unit of measurement (see p. 77).

Chapter 12

Writing to others
Letters and applications

As a student you write not only in preparing your own notes but also to communicate your knowledge and understanding in coursework and examinations. By writing you demonstrate your ability to think.

In any career your value as an employee will depend not only upon your qualifications, experience, and special interests but also upon your ability to communicate information and ideas to other people. You will need to communicate with the people you work for and, as you take on the responsibilities of leadership, you will need to pass on clear instructions to others. But long before this, when applying for admission to a course of study or for employment, writing a good letter will increase your chances of being invited for interview. Such a composition, therefore, although short, may be the most important you ever write.

WRITING A GOOD LETTER

Letter writing may seem far removed from answering questions in coursework and examinations, but these different kinds of writing should have many common characteristics (see the alphabetical list on p. 22).

If you can write a good letter, to obtain just the information you require or provide just the information someone else requires, then you probably appreciate that the first consideration in letter writing – as in any other communication – is what the reader needs to know. When initiating any correspondence, consider what you would like to know, how to make your requirements clear, and how the reader is likely to be affected by your words. Before replying to a letter, consider what must be included, why this information is required, and by whom.

Table 25 Different kinds of letter and their tone

Purpose of letter	Tone
Request for details (of a course of study, an appointment, an item of equipment) *Invitation* to a speaker	Clear, simple, direct, and courteous
Application for employment	Clear, direct and factual. Confident but not aggressive
Complaint	Clear and direct but not aggressive
Reply (to an enquiry or complaint) giving information, instruction or explanation. Reply to all the points raised in the enquiry.	Clear, direct, informative, polite, helpful, and sincere
Acknowledgement (of an enquiry or application) Acknowledgement by postcard	Simple and direct Discreet
Letter of thanks	Appreciative

When you write to people you know, clearly their opinion of you is not entirely based on what and how you write. However, when you write to people whom you have never met they will judge you in the only way they can: by your writing. You should therefore take care over the content, layout, and appearance of any letter to make sure that it makes a favourable impression on the recipient (see Table 25).

The organization of all except the shortest letters can be improved, and their length reduced, if you make a few notes of the points you wish to emphasize and then number them in an effective order. Then, having decided what to say, convey your message simply, clearly, concisely, and courteously. These are the essentials.

Try to put yourself in the place of the recipient as you read your letter before signing it. A good letter is one that creates a favourable impression and enables you to convey information pleasurably, or to obtain the action or information you require.

When you write a business letter, remember there is no special *business English*. The only rule is to avoid words and phrases that you would not use in other kinds of writing (for example, 'I remain your obedient servant', 'Please find enclosed,' and similar outmoded expressions), and to omit superfluous introductory phrases (for example, 'I am writing to let you know that . . .').

Most letters are written on one side of one sheet of paper, so writing letters can provide frequent opportunities to improve your writing without occupying too much of your time.

In a few words you must pass on your message and create the right atmosphere between yourself and the person addressed. The tone of the letter will depend upon your purpose (see Table 25), but no letter should be discourteous.

To keep each communication short and to the point, any necessary supporting details or further information should be referred to briefly but sent as an enclosure.

The initiator of any correspondence should state the purpose of the letter either by a clear, precise, and specific heading, or in the first sentence. However, remember that the heading is not part of the letter and the purpose of the letter should always be made clear in the first sentence, which might begin: 'Please . . .', or 'I should be grateful if . . .'

The reply, and any further correspondence, should have an identical heading and should begin: 'Thank you for your letter of . . . about . . .' From these beginnings both the writer and the recipient know immediately what each communication is about (see Tables 26–29).

Answer every letter promptly. A prompt reply makes for efficiency, enabling you to complete a task, and your courtesy impresses the recipient favourably. Before replying to a letter, read it carefully. Then make sure you answer all the writer's questions. If there is some good reason for delaying your reply, acknowledge receipt of the letter by postcard (see Table 29), and then send your reply as soon as you can.

In business file every letter you receive, with a copy of your reply. Copies are necessary for your own reference, and so that colleagues can see an up-to-date record of all correspondence or deal with any further enquiries if you are unavailable.

Letters have not been superseded by other means of communication. Anything agreed on the telephone must be confirmed in writing, normally on the same day. Misunderstandings are possible unless both parties have an accurate record of their conversation (see Figure 21).

Every letter must fit into the filing system (records) of both the sender and the recipient. It should therefore deal with one subject

Table 26 Layout of a formal business letter

Addresses should not be punctuated. Words such as Company (Co.) and Limited (Ltd.) may be abbreviated. The date should be given in full, without punctuation. The position and address of the recipient must be written as on the envelope. The salutation should be Dear Sir, Dear Sirs or Dear Madam, and the complimentary close: Yours faithfully (or, in the USA, Yours truly). Your signature should be legible. The supporting details, if they are more than a few lines, should be sent on a separate sheet, which should have a title. This and any other enclosures must be listed after the name of the sender under the heading Enclosures.

                                       Address of sender

                                         Date letter is signed
                                         and posted

Position and
address of
recipient

Salutation,

                     Subject heading

     1 Information required

     2 Supporting details

     3 Conclusions and/or action required

       Complimentary close

       Signature

       Typed name and
       position of sender (if the letter is typed)

Enclosures: (List)

Reference line (if the letter is typed): initials of the person signing the letter and those of the typist.

Table 27 Example of a formal business letter

Your address

Date letter is signed
and posted

The Academic Registrar
Name of institution
and full address

Dear Sir,

      Could you please send further particulars of your course in _____ _____. I shall be taking my _____ examinations, in two years time, in the following subjects: _____, _____, and _____ .

      I should be grateful if you would also confirm that these do provide a satisfactory basis for your course, or let me know of any special admission requirements.

Yours faithfully,

only. If you have to write about more than one subject to the same person, each should be dealt with in a separate letter, even if these are enclosed in the same envelope.

Forms of address, to be used on the envelope, are suggested in Table 30. Ensure that the address on the envelope is identical with that used in the letter, because you may need to check, later, from your copy of the letter, that the envelope was correctly addressed. If appropriate, you may wish to write *Personal* or *Confidential* in the top left-hand corner of the envelope.

Table 28 Layout of a less formal business letter

This type of letter is used in business when the correspondents have met or when they know each other well from conversations on the telephone or from previous correspondence. The address should not be punctuated: no words should be abbreviated. The date should be given in full, without punctuation. The salutation includes the surname of the recipient, and the complimentary close is normally Yours sincerely. Your signature should be legible. The name and address of the recipient, as written on the envelope, are in the bottom left-hand corner of the letter.

Address of sender

Date letter is signed
and posted

Salutation,

     1 Information required

     2 Supporting details

     3 Conclusion and/or action required

       Complimentary close

       Signature

       Typed name of sender

Name and address
of recipient

Enclosures: (List)

Reference line: sender's initials and those of the typist.

Table 29 How to use a postcard

A: *Correct use*

                                              Date

Omit salutation

Message: note that a postcard may be seen by other people, as well as by the person addressed. When a postcard is used to acknowledge the receipt of a letter, therefore, the reply should not make public the contents or purpose of the letter: it should include only the date of the letter and, if there is one, a reference number.

Omit complimentary close

The message should be followed immediately by the signature and the typed or printed name and address of the sender.

B: *An example*

                                    Date card is signed

Thank you for your letter of _____ which is receiving attention.

                    Signature of sender

                    Position and
                    address
                    of sender

A reference line may be included, as in a business letter.

'Be ready to take a letter . . .'

Figure 21 In business a letter is usually a more satisfactory means of communication than a telephone conversation (see p. 145)

IMPROVE YOUR WRITING

Applying for employment

Writing a letter is an exercise that most students will find useful and interesting. This is a good place to start teaching or learning the essentials of clear, concise, and courteous writing.

Writing a letter is a test of your ability to communicate effectively – in appropriate language. Write a letter applying for a vacation job or for the kind of work that you would like to do after completing your education. Remember that the way a letter of application is written may cause an employer to conclude that the applicant is not suitable for the job. Whenever you write a business letter, such as an application, take care over its appearance.

1 *Use unlined white paper* (size A4 = 210 × 297 mm).
2 Write legibly or type the letter.

Table 30 Forms of address (to be used on the envelope)

Mr John Smith (if John Smith is an adult)
Mrs John Smith (to John Smith's wife)[1]
John Smith Esq. (if you wish to indicate your respect)
Miss Jean Smith (if Jean Smith is unmarried)[2]
Master John Smith (if John Smith is a child)
John Smith (if John Smith is an adolescent)
Miss Jean Smith, BA PhD or Dr Jean Smith[2]
John Smith Esq., BSc PhD or Dr John Smith[3]
Messrs John Smith & Sons[4]

Note:
1 Some married women, especially if they are in business or the professions, prefer to use their maiden name.
2 In business correspondence a woman should indicate how she wishes to be addressed, for example by typing Miss Jean Smith, Dr Jean Smith or Mrs John Smith, immediately below her signature.
3 A man may type, below his signature, either John Smith or Dr John Smith, but he should not call himself Mr John Smith or John Smith Esq. When Esq. is used, in an address, no other title should stand before the name.
4 The prefix Messrs (French *Messieurs*), as the plural of Mr, is now rarely used in business correspondence. Letters are usually addressed to an individual by name or to The Secretary or The Manager, etc. However, the term Messrs is acceptable in addressing firms with personal names, e.g. Messrs John Smith & Sons. It is not used in addressing limited companies or firms that do not trade under a surname.

For guidance on the correct use of titles and other distinguishing marks of honour or office, see *Titles and Forms of Address*, A. & C. Black, London.

3 Leave adequate margins.
4 Keep a rough copy or, if your letter is typed, keep a carbon copy.
5 Use a white envelope.
6 Fold the paper twice so that it fits neatly into the envelope.

The success of your application, in enabling you to obtain an interview (see p. 155), will depend not only on the care with which you prepare the application but also upon your interests and suitability as indicated in your application.

An application is normally in two parts: (1) a letter of application; and (2) a curriculum vitae (c.v.) on a separate sheet enclosed with your letter (see Tables 31 and 32).

In the letter you ask to be considered for this particular vacancy and you state why you are applying: for example, why you consider that you are suitable and why you think that you would find the work interesting.

In the curriculum vitae, state your name, date of birth, nationality,

Table 31 An example of a letter of application

Your address

Date letter is signed

The Personnel Officer
Name of firm
and full address

Dear Madam

Please consider this application for the post of _____
_____ (Ref. no. _____), advertised in
_____ on _____ _____ _____.

I am just completing an honours degree course in _____
_____ at _____ _____. I was deputy head boy
at school, and have worked in a supermarket and in a factory. I
have also travelled in _____. I enjoy working
with other people and should like to make a career in
_____ _____. I have a particular interest in
_____ _____. My curriculum vitae is enclosed.

I shall be taking my final examinations in _____.
Otherwise, I could come for interview at any time convenient to
you.

Yours faithfully,

---

address, and telephone number. Name your school. List the subjects you studied (or are studying) at school and give the results of any school examinations. Similarly, name your college, list the subjects you are studying, and give the results of any examinations. List your hobbies, clubs, sports, and other non-academic interests. Mention any weekend or vacation work or other work experience, especially if this is relevant to the work for which you are now applying. Give the names of two referees. One of these should be able to speak of your character and non-academic interests, and the other should be a teacher or someone you have worked for

Table 32 An example of a curriculum vitae or résumé

Thomas Jones   Date of birth: 15 January 1990
British
Single
Home address:
Telephone no.

2001–8 _____ High School, _____, _____
    2006 _____ examination results
        English   B   Science   C
        History   C   Mathematics   B
        Geography   A   French   A

2008 _____ examination results
        English   A
        History   B   Further mathematics   B
        Economics   B

2008– _____ University
    Studying English, economics and mathematics.
    Reading for honours degree in economics.
    Final examinations in June 2011.
    Non-academic interests. At school I was deputy head
    boy and played rugby for the 1st XV. At university I play
    squash for the 2nd team. I enjoy reading, listening to
    music and going to the theatre. In the school holidays I
    worked in a supermarket. I travelled in _____
    in the summer of 2009, and had a labouring job with
    _____ _____ for 8 weeks in the summer
    of 2010.

Referees   _____   _____
            Personnel Manager   Senior Lecturer
            _____ _____   Department of Economics
            _____   _____ University
            _____   _____

                        (Sign and date) ....

recently. Choose your referees carefully, *for each application*, to make
sure they are appropriate, and remember to ask their permission
before you give their names.

Include dates in your curriculum vitae (see Table 32), so that it is a summary of all the important events and achievements in your life that are likely to interest *this employer*. Ensure that every year is properly accounted for: otherwise the employer may wonder if you have something to hide.

As in any other composition, consider your readers. If the post has been advertised some details will be given in the advertisement. You may then write for further details and an application form (which you should use instead of a curriculum vitae). The further details will tell you more about the post advertised and about the employer.

If you have to complete an application form, first read it carefully and prepare your answers to the questions on separate sheets. Copy them on to the form when you are satisfied that they are the best answers that you can give. Be careful to obey any instructions. For example, you may be asked to write in black ink or to answer certain questions in block capitals. You must answer all the questions, even if you write only *none* or *not applicable*.

It is best to make corrections and improvements on a first draft of your application until you are satisfied that you know how best to present yourself. Then, if there is time, put the draft on one side for a few days. Read it again and try to think how the recipient will react. Imagine that the reader will be middle-aged, and that he or she is looking for someone with respect for authority, with a positive personality, who is likely to get along well with other people and accept responsibility. You may ask a friend to read your application.

Either have your application typed *or* write it again, legibly and neatly (see pp. 2 and 150). Post it to arrive before the closing date. Keep a copy for reference.

Making the most of yourself in an application is clearly a time-consuming job, but it is worth spending several hours on this task if you are trying to obtain suitable employment for a whole vacation or possibly for the rest of your working life.

Chapter 13

Speaking for yourself

ASKING QUESTIONS

When you take notes in a lesson or lecture, note particularly anything that you do not fully understand or any aspect about which you would like further information. You may mark these by a question mark in the margin, so that when the time comes you are ready to ask questions (see Table 3, p. 18). Some teachers like to clarify any possible misunderstandings or to answer any relevant questions as they go along; others prefer to wait until the end.

Get into the habit of asking questions. Good questions help to keep everyone attentive and to stimulate thought.

Rewriting notes can be a waste of time (see p. 13). However, read carefully through your notes to make sure that you understand them and that there are no gaps. If necessary look at your textbook or try to find the answers to your questions from other sources of information (see Chapter 9). If any questions remain or if you require further information, you will be ready to ask questions at the next opportunity.

ANSWERING QUESTIONS: BEING INTERVIEWED

Before an interview for a place at college or for a job, find out as much as you can about the course or the employer — and about the selection procedures used. This is very important: it is something that could influence the success of your interview — and so the rest of your life. The more you know, the better you will be able to talk about the work that will be expected of you. You will be able to ask sensible questions. Remember that in a short time the interviewers have to decide how interested you are, and how enthusiastic, and how well qualified. They have to make judgements about your personality.

When you attend an interview, your appearance and attitude are as important as what you say. You are most likely to be interviewed by middle-aged people who, after years of experience, have reached positions of responsibility. Your dress and language should be appropriate for the occasion. You must not arrive late.

Before the formal interview, if you are given a guided tour of the premises or shown equipment, you may be asked questions and have the opportunity to ask intelligent questions, to display your interest, and so to create a favourable first impression. Learn as much as you can from your conversations and observations.

When the time comes for your interview, walk confidently into the room. Do not sit until you are invited to do so. Sit up so that your clothes look good and so that you feel comfortable, self-confident, and alert. Conversation in an interview is likely to be formal and not immediately relaxed; but a good interviewer will help you to feel at ease and will make any necessary introductions.

You are likely to be asked, first, for your name. This is to make sure that you are the person expected at this time. You may then be asked to confirm other details given in your application, such as when and where you were born and where you were educated. Answering such factual questions gives you time to relax a little. Speak clearly and use your normal speaking voice. As in normal conversation, look at the person or persons you are addressing and do not be afraid to smile occasionally. Show your interest and enthusiasm.

Listen carefully to the questions and try to give short and straightforward answers to any simple questions. However, do not feel that you have to respond immediately to every question. If you feel that a few moments of thought will help you to give a more complete and sensible answer, allow yourself a little time. Try to summarize your thoughts when a question calls for a longer reply, so that you do not talk for too long at a time. The interviewer can ask further questions if more detail is required.

If you write in your application (see p. 150) or in your curriculum vitae (see Table 32) that you have certain interests, you must expect to be asked questions about these subjects. Your answers will indicate the extent of your interest — and how enthusiastic you are. So look through your application when you are preparing for the interview. This should help you to anticipate certain questions and to consider your replies. For example, if you have done project work you may be asked questions about what you did; and if you have had a period of vacation employment or a training year, you are likely to be asked how you feel you benefited from the experience. See also Table 33.

Be prepared, during the interview, to take opportunities to draw attention to those interests and experiences that you particularly wish the interviewer or the interviewing committee to know about. Volunteer such information at appropriate points, but try not to give the impression that you are boasting or that you are conducting the interview.

Towards the end of the interview you will almost certainly be asked if you have any questions. Be prepared for this. Think before the interview and, if necessary, make a note of one or two questions that you would particularly like to ask. If you are seeking employment, the starting salary will probably already have been made clear but you may wish to ask about training opportunities and promotion prospects.

Do not hesitate to speak if you find that the person chairing the meeting is closing the interview without asking if there is anything you wish to say or any questions you wish to ask. He or she may just not care whether or not you have any questions, or may have forgotten to ask: in either case you have nothing to lose.

TAKING PART IN A TUTORIAL

In a tutorial you may have the opportunity to discuss with a tutor, and perhaps with a few students, your plan for an essay or your thoughts expressed in a completed essay. At least, you should know in advance what subject is to be discussed. You should then prepare for the tutorial.

Given a title, you can prepare a plan – similar to a topic outline for an essay. In this your thoughts on the subject are organized, so that in the tutorial you will have something to say. Then leave plenty of space in your plan so that you can add relevant ideas contributed by others. Listen carefully; then make your comments brief but to the point. Ask for clarification. Ask other questions. Criticize and comment. If you use tutorials and other discussion groups in this way, you will learn both from your preparation and from the discussion.

Table 33 Possible sequence of questions and answers at the beginning of an interview

Possible questions	Possible replies
Good morning, Mr Jones, my name is Mrs Telford. I am the Product Development Manager.	Good morning, Mrs Telford.
Please sit down.	Thank you.
As you know, we are here today to interview applicants for . . . I should just like to confirm a few details from your application.	
1 I see that you are twenty-one.	Yes, I am.
You went to school in . . .	Yes.
Note: There will probably be other factual questions (e.g. about the subjects you have studied, and about vacation work or other employment).	
2 I see that you are keen on sport.	Yes, Mrs Telford. I play cricket in my summer vacations for . . . I am a spin bowler.
What is it about cricket that appeals to you?	*Note*: By this time the interviewer has already found out quite a lot about you. Your answer to this open-ended question will tell him much more about your personality.
3 You say in your application that you like reading.	Yes, I read for relaxation.
What kind of books do you prefer?	I read novels mostly,
Who are your favourite authors?	*Note*: If you have nothing to say at this stage the interviewer will conclude that you are not, after all, interested in reading.
What is it that you like about the novels by . . .?	
4 Tell me, Mr Jones, why did you apply for a place on this course/vacation work with us/a training place here/this vacancy?	*Note*: This is something that you should have considered before preparing your application. You should therefore be ready with an intelligent and enthusiastic reply.

Possible questions	Possible replies
5 What qualities do you feel you have that make you suited to this post?	*Note*: Be prepared for such a question, which will give you the opportunity to state, positively, why you consider you would make a success of the job.

PREPARING FOR A SEMINAR

If you attend a seminar you will know what subject is to be discussed. You can make preparations, as for a tutorial.

If you are asked to introduce the subject for discussion at a seminar, remember that if the whole seminar is to take thirty minutes your introduction must not take more than ten. Before the seminar, prepare a plan of what you wish to say. Out of ten minutes you may spend two on introducing the subject. You will then have just enough time to refer briefly to two or three aspects upon which you consider the discussion should be concentrated. Inexperienced speakers usually try to make too many points and to support their arguments with too much detail – with the result that they run out of time.

If you have not given a seminar previously, you will find it helpful to tell someone what you are planning to say. By doing this you will learn, before the seminar, how little you are able to say in the time available.

The best seating plan for a seminar is one in which the participants are in a circle, perhaps around a table. Everyone should make brief notes while other people are talking. Make a note of what is being said and of things you may wish to contribute to the discussion. Because the time for the discussion is short, all questions and answers and comments should be concise.

During the seminar, look at people whenever you are talking. Look around to make sure that everyone is listening, and speak clearly so that they all hear every word.

GIVING A TALK

Teachers find that they learn most about their subject, and learn quickly and easily, when they have to teach others. Teachers may therefore encourage students to prepare for a tutorial, or to introduce a seminar, or to deliver a short talk: these are effective methods of instruction.

However, even if you do not have the opportunity to give a talk as part of your coursework, you may wish to speak at meetings, or to give short talks at clubs, or you may have to talk to a group of people after you have completed your education – for example, as part of an employer's selection procedure which may last several days, or as part of your employment when you may have to give instruction as part of a training course.

Preparing and planning

Consider your audience and ask yourself: What do I wish to achieve in the time available?

1 Make sure that you know enough about the subject. Do any necessary background reading. You must be self-confident if you are to gain the confidence of your audience.
2 Decide on a limited number of main points that you must make. Arrange these in an appropriate sequence and then check that they are all essential in relation to your aim.
3 You may find it helpful to make a note of each main point on an index card or at the top of a blank sheet of paper – with any essential supporting details or evidence summarized below each heading.
4 The number of main points that can be made in the time available, and the amount of supporting detail required, will depend upon your audience. What prior knowledge, if any, can you assume to be shared by all members of your audience?
5 Consider what visual aids, if any, are required to support your words. For example, decide which words are most important (these are your main headings) and which words may be new to some members of your audience, so that you will remember to write these words on a blackboard, whiteboard or overhead projector.
6 Prepare any necessary stores, equipment or visual aids; and decide exactly when you are going to use them to support your words and to add interest. See *Visual aids*, p. 162.
7 Plan any demonstration that will reinforce your words and add interest.
8 Try to make your talk interesting. Doing so depends upon (a)

your knowledge of the subject and your ability to select what is relevant to this talk; (b) showing that what you have to say is relevant to the needs of this audience – that it follows on from their existing interests or that it will help them in some other way; (c) ensuring variety and simplicity in presentation; (d) letting people see as well as hear (see visual aids); and (e) avoiding distractions.

9 To make sure that you can finish on time, it is a good idea to go through your talk beforehand, by yourself or with a friend. Remember that you will need to leave time for questions (see *Delivery*, below).

10 Ensure that the room to be used for your talk is the right size and that the equipment you need will be available and in working order.

Delivery

If possible, ensure that the room is warm enough and well ventilated. Try to ensure that no one can see out of a window or hear distracting noises. Stand where everyone can see you, but avoid distracting mannerisms such as juggling with chalk, swinging or banging a pointer, or constantly walking to and fro.

1 Speak so that everyone can hear every word. Try not to speak in a monotone. Look around your audience to capture everyone's attention. Maintain eye contact so that you can appreciate the needs of individuals – to see that they do understand. Show your enthusiasm for the subject.

2 If possible, do not read your talk. Use your notes as reminders.

3 Make sure that everyone knows who you are!

4 Say what you are going to talk about. Remind the audience how this follows on from what they already know. Give the reason for your talk. Define your aim. This is your opportunity, in your introduction, to capture attention and promote a desire to listen.

5 In the body of your talk make each of your main points clearly and in an effective order. Pause briefly after each main point has been made, to let everyone know that it is time to start thinking about something else.

6 To ensure that you keep their attention, it is a good idea to give your audience something to do. For example, you may write a word on a blackboard or use some other visual aid to reinforce a

main point. They then have something to see as well as something to hear. Or you may ask a question of your audience from time to time — to make them consider something that you want them to consider. Then pause briefly to give everyone time to think before you *either* answer the question yourself *or* invite one person, by name, to attempt an answer.

7 At the end of your talk, summarize each of your main points and state clearly what conclusions you draw. Say why they may be important for your audience.

8 Leave time for questions. In teaching, questions should be asked at this stage — to enable you to *confirm* that everyone has understood and remembered your main points and your conclusions. Whether or not it is appropriate for you to ask questions, you should always invite questions. Questions from your audience may *reveal misunderstandings*, or may enable you to make *additional relevant points* that you were unable to include in your talk, or may provide a basis for an interesting *discussion*. Therefore, if your talk is for thirty minutes, you may decide to speak for twenty minutes and to leave ten minutes for questions.

   If you are asked a question, repeat the question to make sure that everyone knows exactly what the question is. Then keep your answer short, clear and to the point.

9 *Finish on time.*

VISUAL AIDS

Using a blackboard or whiteboard

If you know how to use a blackboard or whiteboard properly, you will be able to prepare effective visual aids quickly at the most appropriate times during your talks.

1 On a green or black board use yellow or white chalk. Remember that only pastel shades will show up on a dark board. On a whiteboard use black or dark red, green or blue — but not yellow.

2 Spell any word that may be new to some people in your audience in clear block capitals.

3 Use clear, simple diagrams that can be constructed quickly; you should plan them before your talk.

4 When you turn away from your audience to draw or write, always stop talking.

5 Try not to obscure anyone's view either while you are drawing or afterwards.
6 Give people time to study any diagram quietly, without the distracting effect of your voice.
7 Keep the board clean. Do not allow people to continue looking at things you have finished talking about – once you are trying to interest them in something else.

Using an overhead projector

As with a blackboard, or any other equipment, you will find an overhead projector most useful if you have considered, beforehand, how best to use it.

1 Prefer dark inks on a white screen.
2 Prepare tables and diagrams and then project them before your talk – so that you can check, from the back of the room, that they are all clear and that you have not included too much detail or anything irrelevant.
3 If you write during your talk, make sure that the lines are distinct and that the words are legible. As with a blackboard, spell any word that may be new to some people in your audience.
4 Use a pointer so that you can point at the screen. Do not point at the transparency *with your finger* – this obscures the view.
5 However, you may find it helpful to obscure part of a table or diagram deliberately (with a card) so that you can use just the part that is required at the time.
6 When you write or draw, stop talking. And remember that people may need time to study a table or diagram quietly.
7 Remove each transparency as soon as it has served its purpose.
8 Look at your audience when you speak. Try to make sure that they are looking at what you wish them to see.
9 When you speak, stand away from the projector – next to your notes.

SOME TIPS ON TALKING

1 First get into the habit of asking questions (see p. 155). This will help you to gain confidence. All you have to do is to ask the question, and then listen.
2 In a tutorial, agree with your tutor, and with other students, the

topics for the paragraphs of an essay. Each topic word or sentence should then be written on a separate index card. The cards should then be shuffled and dealt, upside down, one to each student — as in a card game. Each student in turn is asked to look at his or her card and to speak on the topic, without preparation, for one minute (or longer as the participants become more confident).

Word processing

USING A WORD PROCESSOR

1 Before using a word processor you are advised to learn touch typing so that you can type fast enough to maintain a train of thought. Otherwise, you will have to handwrite at least your first draft of any composition to allow your thoughts and written words to flow. Then, if necessary, you can word-process your second draft.

2 If you do not know how to use a word processor and can learn as part of your course of study, take full advantage of the opportunity.

3 If a training package is provided for a word processor with which you are not familiar, it is a good idea to work through this several times.

4 The facilities available differ from one word processor to another. Your computer (and printer) may not be able to support all the facilities a particular word-processing package can provide. You must ensure, therefore, that the requirements of the recipient of any document you are to prepare, in relation to its format (for example, layout of headings, spacing of lines, numbering of pages, and types of illustration), can be met by the computer and printer, and word-processing software, you plan to purchase or to use.

If you are thinking of purchasing a word-processing package you are advised not to do so until (a) you have considerable experience of word processing, (b) you know what your requirements are likely to be on the course for which you have enrolled, and (c) you can purchase one that is compatible with your college software.

For your work as a student, monospace founts are recommended because they are less likely than proportional founts to cause problems with formatting.

Make sure that the word processor produces graphs of an acceptable standard (for example, with the axes correctly labelled and with appropriate scales).

It is advantageous to choose a word processor and printer that use the same page description language (for example, PostScript (a registered trademark of Adobe Systems Inc.)).

Because of rapid advances in computer technology, the longer you wait before purchasing a word processor package the more you are likely to obtain for your money, or the less you are likely to have to pay for a particular package.

5 With some word processors, formatting commands are selected as you write the document, with the result that if you decide later to alter, for example, the way section headings are to appear, you have to change them all – one at a time. With better word processors, however, you may be able to decide on the format of a document, before starting to write, by using a separate style specification. You could decide, for example, how section headings were to appear in a project report. Then you would have to identify section headings as such, as you typed – and when the report was printed these headings would all appear according to the formatting instructions in the style specification. This facility allows you to prepare long documents more quickly, and you need change only the format of the section headings in the style specification, for example, to alter the appearance of all the section headings in the document.

6 In word processing, keyboard keys are used to enter the text for a document as well as to send word processing commands to the word processor – unless a mouse is being used. A major difficulty is that different word processors have different sets of commands. So if you know how to use one, you may make mistakes when using another. Even if commands are identical, they are likely to be implemented by pressing different keys or selecting different items in different menus. Also, different word processors use different conventions when displaying formatting information on a visual display unit. Because it is not possible to give detailed instructions or advice, this appendix includes only general advice: the term word processing is used throughout for both word processing and desktop publishing.

HOW A WORD PROCESSOR CAN HELP YOU

If you know how to use a word processor, and have good keyboard skills, word processing can help you in all four stages of composition – thinking, planning, writing, and revising – and enable you to prepare a long document, for example an extended essay, dissertation, or project report, more easily and quickly than would otherwise have been possible.

You can produce a document with a print quality similar to that of a book and, for example, you can print in italics the words that in a handwritten composition should be underlined (see p. 92), and you can print words in bold. However, you are advised: (a) to check with your supervisor or assessor that italics are acceptable, because underlining may still be preferred, (b) to use bold for sub-headings when necessary, but not to emphasize words in the text by printing them in bold or placing them in inverted commas, (c) not to underline words for emphasis, and (d) not to underline headings; it is enough to give them a line to themselves as on this page.

Before you write

A word processor allows you to prepare a topic outline, on the screen, and then add material under relevant headings. Instead of writing on paper, as you think about what should be included in your composition, you enter information using the keyboard (and mouse). The words appear on the screen, and you can rearrange them if necessary as you decide how to organize your work. But you must still think and prepare a topic outline or plan before you type your composition (for all the reasons stated on p. 36), just as you would if you were using a pen.

As you write

A word processor:

1 automatically formats text;
2 may provide a choice of founts (print styles and sizes) and different attributes (for example, bold);
3 inserts running headings and page numbers, as in a book (see above), reducing the work involved in preparing a long composition;
4 may enable you to check spelling, syntax, and grammar;

5 may provide advice on the choice of words (see Chapter 5) and
   on the use of words (see Chapter 6);
6 may provide a thesaurus.

After writing

You can check, correct, and if necessary revise your work, without
the alterations being apparent to the reader, and without your
having to retype whole pages of text, and then you can produce an
attractive printout. This means that traditional cut-and-paste techniques, involving the retyping of whole pages or whole documents,
are replaced by a limitless electronic cut-and-paste facility.

Some word processors require you to leave spaces so that you
can insert your own illustrations later. Others allow you to insert
either simple diagrams that may be drawn using the word processor,
or illustrations produced using other compatible software, as you
prepare the document.

It may also be possible to enter data in a table and then, with
compatible software, use the word processor to produce pie charts
and other kinds of graphs from these data. You must still decide
how to present information: in the text, in a table, or in a diagram,
but once only (see p. 78). A student should not score extra marks
for presenting the same information in different ways in the same
document (see p. 36), and should score fewer marks because repetition indicates lack of thought on the part of the writer and wastes
the reader's time.

HOW YOU MUST HELP YOURSELF WHEN USING A WORD PROCESSOR

1 Some users think of a word processor as a tool that eliminates
   the need for thinking and planning before writing, and for care
   in writing, because it is easy to correct and revise work later.
   They are wrong.

   Like a pencil, pen, or typewriter, a word processor is an
   instrument you can use to record digits, letters, punctuation
   marks, and other symbols. To combine these symbols, in preparing useful personal records and effective communications, you
   must prepare every composition in four stages. Think and plan
   before you write (see Chapter 4), choose and arrange words
   carefully as you write (see Chapters 5, 6, and 8), to ensure you

express your thoughts simply and clearly, and meet all other requirements of scholarly writing (summarized in Chapter 3), and then check, correct, and if necessary revise your composition (see Chapters 4 and 11).

Remember that a composition can be well presented without its being typed or word-processed (see p. 40). There should not be much wrong with your first draft. If there is, nothing you can do in checking and revising a composition can compensate for your having given insufficient thought to the needs of the reader, or for your failure to plan your work, before starting to write.

This is true whether your composition is handwritten or word-processed. The computer has a memory but no intelligence. It can help you with your work, but you must still do the thinking at each stage in composition. To an assessor or employer your completed compositions, as a student or employee, are an indication of your knowledge, your understanding, and your ability to organize your thoughts in an effective composition that is a good answer to the question set or that keeps within your terms of reference and provides the information required by the reader clearly, simply, concisely, and in an acceptable form.

2 Because with electronic cut-and-paste you do not have to retype a document after revising it, as you would when using traditional cut-and-paste, the result may be a lazily revised composition with duplicated text, and with sentences or paragraphs and cross-references that are out of place. Had the final document been retyped, these faults would have been noticed by a competent typist. Therefore, always check your work carefully and, if possible, ask someone who has an understanding of the work to read any important document — as well as checking it yourself. Instructions should be checked first by yourself, second by someone with knowledge of the task, and third by someone else who may be expected to use them.

3 Although a spell checker ensures that a word is spelt correctly, it does not ensure that it is the right word (see p. 51). Even if it is, the spelling will be either British English or American English and so may be unacceptable to some users. See also Appendix 2.

4 Do not allow a spell checker to spell-check and change, automatically, the names of people or places, technical terms, abbreviations, acronyms, or mnemonics, unless these are in a spell-check dictionary.

5 Before using the word processor for the first time, ensure that it has up-to-date virus-detecting and virus-removing software installed.

6 Before using a disk for the first time ensure that it is checked for viruses, with an up-to-date virus checker.

7 Find out who is responsible for making backup copies of your files or if you must do this yourself.

8 When producing a new document use a new disk and backup disk just for that document.

9 As you correct or revise a document, save (or file) your work from time to time so that, for example, a power failure would not cause you to lose much time.

10 Save your work before you try any new commands if there is any possibility that you may lose or inadvertently alter part or all of the document, so that you can quit (that is, leave the document in its original state) and try again.

11 Each day, when you revise the document, make a new copy using a different file name (for example, the year, month, and day). If the revision takes more than a few days, take weekly backups on separate disks, and if it takes several weeks take monthly backups on separate disks. *Note*: Disks are inexpensive, whereas your time spent re-entering lost information – if this were possible – would cost much more and would interfere with your other work.

12 Label your disks consecutively (for example with your initials and a number: ABC001, ABC002, etc.) and maintain a small hardback notebook as a log of your disks. Record what each disk contains, and for backup disks record the type of backup (daily, weekly, or monthly).

13 When the document is complete, copy it into your master archive disk, and backup archive disk, in case you need copies later, or need to update the document, or include parts in another document.

14 Reformat your document disk ready for your next document.

15 Do not carry all your disks around at one time. Keep your master archive and master backup disks in separate places.

16 You are advised not to use a word processor for all your written assignments. If you do, you may find it very difficult to do your best work in examinations. In coursework spend more time in thinking and planning than you can spare in an examination, but try to actually write at least the first draft of each composition

in about the time that would be available for answering a similar question in an examination – when you will not be able to use a word processor. You must develop your ability to get things right first time in handwritten compositions (see p. 37), even if in coursework you need to prepare a second draft using a typewriter or word processor. However, if you can prepare a first handwritten draft that does not need to be revised, do not waste your time preparing a second draft with a word processor just to change your handwriting into print (see p. 40).

Punctuation

Some people suggest that mistakes in grammar and punctuation do not matter if the writer's meaning is clear. But if the English is poor the meaning is unlikely to be clear. For example:

> This latest outbreak of violence has not surprisingly received the condemnation of politicians of all parties.

To make clear whether or not the rioting has been condemned, commas are needed in the above sentence – after surprisingly and *either* before *or* after not.

USING PUNCTUATION MARKS TO MAKE YOUR MEANING CLEAR

In writing, punctuation marks indicate pauses – and other characteristics of speech – which help to make your meaning clear.

> The Prime Minister said, 'The Leader of the Opposition is a fool.'

> 'The Prime Minister', said the Leader of the Opposition, 'is a fool.'

The meaning of one of these sentences is the opposite of that of the other, but the words, and the order of these words, are identical. Only the punctuation marks are different.

If you have difficulty with punctuation you will find it easiest to write short sentences.

> A sentence expresses a whole thought. It therefore makes sense by itself. A sentence begins with a capital letter. It includes a verb (see Table 34). It ends with a full stop.

Each of these five sentences tells the reader one thing about a

Table 34 Parts of speech: classifying words

Parts of speech	The work words do in a sentence
Verbs	Words that indicate action: what is done, or what was done, or what is said to be. The ship *sailed*.
Nouns	Names. *Nelson* sailed in this *ship*.
Pronouns	Words used instead of nouns so that nouns need not be repeated. *He* sailed in *her*.
Adjectives	Words that describe or qualify nouns or pronouns. The *big* ship sailed across the *shallow* sea.
Adverbs	Words that modify verbs, adjectives and other adverbs. The big ship sailed *slowly* across the *gently* rolling sea.
Prepositions	Each preposition governs, and marks the relation between, a noun or pronoun and some other word in the sentence. The ship sailed *across* the sea *to* America.
Conjunctions	Words used to join the parts of a sentence, or to make two sentences into one. The ship went to America *and* came straight back.

sentence, but note that if you write only in short sentences your reader has no sooner started each sentence than it is time to stop.

USING PUNCTUATION MARKS TO ENSURE THE SMOOTH FLOW OF LANGUAGE

Instead of the five short sentences, the same thoughts could be expressed in two:

A sentence expresses a whole thought: it makes sense by itself. Every sentence starts with a capital letter, includes a verb, and ends with a full stop.

In different sentences you may use the same words to express different thoughts.

Help! You can help. Can you help?

Conversely, in different sentences you may use different words to convey the same thought.

Come! You come. Come here, you!

USING CONJUNCTIONS TO CONTRIBUTE TO THE SMOOTH FLOW OF LANGUAGE

Conjunctions (and, or, but, for, nor, when, which, because) can be used to join parts of a sentence or to make two sentences into one (Table 34). They link closely related thoughts, give continuity to your writing, and help your readers along. However, use each conjunction intelligently and, if possible, not more than once in a sentence.

Remember, also, that some conjunctions must be used in pairs: *both* is always followed by *and*, *either* by *or*, *neither* by *nor*, and *not only* by *but also*.

USING CAPITAL LETTERS

Capital initial letters are used for the first word in a sentence or heading, for most words in the titles of publications (see p. 186), for proper nouns (proper names), for interjections, and for most abbreviations (see p. 59); for example, His church is St Ann's Church.

For emphasis (see p. 111) a whole word may be written in capitals, but initial capital letters are no longer used for this purpose (but see p. 66).

In handwriting a clear distinction should be made between capitals and other letters; and (except possibly in a signature) capitals should not be used as an embellishment.

PUNCTUATION MARKS THAT END A SENTENCE

Use no more punctuation marks than are necessary to make your meaning clear. If you find punctuation difficult, begin by mastering the use of the full stop and keep your sentences short and to the point.

Full stop, exclamation mark, and question mark

The end of a sentence is indicated by a full stop, exclamation mark or question mark.

You must go. Go! Must you go?

Remember that a question mark is used only after a direct question.

Could you explain, please?

I should appreciate an explanation.

I wonder if I should ask for an explanation.

PUNCTUATION MARKS USED WITHIN A SENTENCE

Punctuation marks used to separate the parts of a sentence make the reader pause for a shorter time than does a full stop. The more you read and write, the more you will come to appreciate their value.

Comma

Items in a list may be separated by commas, as in the next sentence. To write clear, concise, and easily read prose we use commas, semicolons, colons, dashes, and parentheses. In such a list the comma before the final *and* is essential only if it contributes to clarity.

A comma may also be used to separate the parts (or clauses) in a sentence. The word clause comes from the Latin word *claudere*, to close, and within a sentence commas may be needed to separate (close off) one thought or statement from the next.

A sentence comprising one clause, expressing one thought, is called a simple sentence. It makes one statement.

Each word should contribute to the sentence.

Each sentence should contribute to the paragraph.

Each paragraph should contribute to the composition.

Nothing should be superfluous.

However, a sentence may comprise more than one clause – expressing more than one thought. A comma or a conjunction, or both, may then be inserted between the separate statements.

Each word should contribute to the sentence, each sentence to the paragraph, and each paragraph to the composition. Nothing should be superfluous.

Note that in this example, at the beginning of the second clause the conjunction (and) is understood: there is no need to write it. Similarly, in each clause there is a verb but in the second and third clauses this verb (contribute) is understood.

Use commas to mark separate clauses if they make for easy reading and help you to convey your thoughts. A commenting clause should be enclosed by commas; a defining clause should not be.

People, who go to church on Sundays, are . . .

People who go to church on Sundays are . . .

Note the difference in meaning. The first sentence implies that all people go to church on Sundays. The second sentence identifies or defines which people are referred to: those who do go.

Do not add commas at random because you feel that a sentence is too long to be without punctuation marks. Either put the comma in the right place, to convey your meaning, or write the sentence so that your meaning is conveyed clearly without the comma.

You will be informed, if you send a stamped addressed envelope, after the meeting.

You will be informed, if you send a stamped addressed envelope after the meeting.

If you send a stamped addressed envelope you will be informed after the meeting.

Note that the first and third sentences convey the same message; one with commas and the other without.

Dashes and parentheses

Dashes and parentheses (curved brackets) may be used — in pairs — when an aside is added to a sentence. So if you removed the asides from the last sentence you would be left with a complete sentence. The asides are said to be in parenthesis. *Parentheses* are used when you wish to insert a cross reference (see p. 79), an example (see p. 92), or an explanation (see p. 86). *Dashes* are used to give prominence to an important insertion. But note that the dashes could be replaced by commas, as in this sentence, if you wished to give less prominence to an aside.

One dash may be used if the aside is added at the end of a sentence — as in this sentence. See also square brackets, p. 178.

Colon

Note the use of a colon to introduce either a list (see p. 6) or a quotation (see p. 2). A colon may also be used, in place of a full stop, either (a) between two statements of equal weight (see p. 16), or (b) between two statements if the second is an explanation or elaboration of the first (see p. 27).

Semicolon

The full stop (or period), the colon, the semicolon, the dash, the comma, and bracket are all punctuation marks, points, or stops. They are here placed in order. The full stop gives the longest and most impressive pause. The semicolon, which gives a longer pause than a comma and a shorter pause than a colon, may contribute to clarity (see pages 27, 46, 89, 90 and 92).

OTHER PUNCTUATION MARKS

Apostrophe

First, note that an apostrophe is *never used* in forming the plural: apple becomes apples; criterion, criteria; datum, data; gateau, gateaux; lady, ladies; man, men; mouse, mice; phenomenon, phenomena; and wife, wives.

Then note that if you avoid colloquial English (see p. 63), you will use an apostrophe *or* a possessive adjective *or* a possessive pronoun only when you wish to indicate that someone or something belongs to someone or something (see pp. 182–3).

Quotation marks

You may use quotation marks when you quote someone's words exactly (see pp. 15 and 76). However, this is not the only way to signpost quotations. For example, in this book extracts are clearly marked in the headings of some tables (see p. 63), or they are marked by indentation (see pp. 2–3). Note that quotation marks are included if they are part of the extract: otherwise they are hardly used in this book. Many authors now manage without them.

When quoting someone else's work, the part quoted must be complete – including every word and every punctuation mark. Any gaps in the quotation should be indicated by dots (as on p. 3) and any words you insert must be indicated by square brackets (as on p. 3).

The source of each quotation should normally be acknowledged (see p. 2), unless you have some good reason for not doing so (e.g. see pp. 23–4). See also pp. 35–6.

The use of quotation marks to indicate that a word or phrase is not to be understood in its usual sense is to be avoided, because the intended sense may not be clear to the reader. Instead, choose words that convey your meaning precisely (see p. 51).

The titles of books, plays, and poems should not be marked by quotation marks, as is sometimes recommended, but by underlining (or, in print, by italics – see p. 92). Use underlining to help you to distinguish, for example, between David Copperfield (the name of a character in a book) and David Copperfield (the name of the book).

IMPROVE YOUR WRITING

The best way to appreciate the usefulness of different punctuation marks is to study one or two pages of any book or article that interests you. Consider why the author has used each punctuation mark. You can repeat this exercise with as many compositions as you choose to study. In writing clear and simple English you can manage without semicolons and colons, but as you begin to appreciate their value you will want to use them.

Spelling

You may think, if you spell badly, that poor spelling does not matter. However, mistakes in spelling, as with mistakes in punctuation and grammar, reduce an educated reader's confidence in a writer. Mistakes in spelling also distract readers, taking their attention away from the writer's meaning. Spelling correctly, therefore, is part of efficient communication — as well as being good manners.

SOME REASONS FOR POOR SPELLING

Some words are not spelt as they are pronounced: e.g. answer (anser), gauge (gage), island (iland), mortgage (morgage), psychology (sycology), rough (ruff), sugar (shugar), and tongue (tung). You cannot, therefore, spell all words just as you pronounce them. This is one problem for people who find spelling difficult.

However, those who speak badly are likely to find that incorrect pronunciation does lead to incorrect spelling. In lazy speech secretary becomes secatary; environment, enviroment; police, pleece; computer, compu'er; and so on. If you know that you speak and spell badly, take more care over your speech.

Unfortunately, the speech of teachers and radio or TV announcers does not necessarily provide a reliable guide to pronunciation. Consult a dictionary, therefore, if you are unsure of the pronunciation or spelling of any word. And whenever you have to consult a dictionary to see how a word is spelt, check the pronunciation at the same time. Knowing how to pronounce the word correctly, you may have no further difficulty in spelling it correctly.

If you do not read very much, you give yourself few opportunities for increasing your vocabulary (see Chapter 6) and for seeing words spelt correctly. Reading effective prose (see pp. 19 and 97) will help you in these and other ways.

SOME RULES TO REMEMBER

The best way to improve your spelling is to consult a dictionary and then to memorize the correct spelling of any word that you find you have spelt incorrectly. However, learning the following rules — one at a time — will also help.

1   Remember this rule. When **ie** or **ei** are pronounced **ee**, the *i* comes before the **e** except after **c** (as in believe and receive).
    Notes. Seize and species are exceptions to this rule.
        The **ei** is not pronounced **ee** in eight, either, foreign, freight, reign, weight, and weir.

2   When words ending in *fer* are made longer (for example when refer is used in making the longer words reference and referred), the *r* is not doubled if, in pronouncing the longer word, you stress the first syllable (as in **ref**erence), but it is doubled if you stress the second syllable (as in re**ferred**).

    A *syllable* is a unit of pronunciation which forms a word or part of a word.

	First stress (r)	*Second stress (rr)*
defer	**defer**ence	de**ferr**ed, de**ferr**ing
differ	**diff**erence, **diff**ering	
infer	**infer**ence	in**ferr**ed, in**ferr**ing
offer	**off**ered, **off**ering	
refer	**refer**ee, **refer**ence	re**ferr**ed, re**ferr**ing
suffer	**suff**ering, **suff**erance	
transfer	**trans**ference	trans**ferr**ed, trans**ferr**ing

3   With verbs of more than one syllable that end with a single vowel (*a, e, i, o* or *u*) followed by a single consonant (a letter that is not a vowel), in forming the past tense or a present or past participle double the consonant if the last syllable is stressed.
There are exceptions to this rule, including funnel (funnelled), model (modelled), panel (panelled), rival (rivalled), travel (travelled) and tunnel (tunnelled). See exercise 2 on p. 184.

	First stress (one consonant)	Second stress (two consonants)
benefit	benefited, benefiting	
bias	biased	
control		controlled, controlling
excel		excelled, excelling
focus	focused, focusing	
parallel	paralleled	
refer		referred, referring

4 With verbs of one syllable that end with a single vowel followed by a single consonant, double the consonant before adding *ing*.

run	running
sag	sagging
swim	swimming
whip	whipping

On the other hand, if a verb of one syllable does not end in a single vowel followed by a single consonant, simply add *ing*.

daub	daubing
deal	dealing
feel	feeling
help	helping
sink	sinking
watch	watching

5 When verbs ending in *e* are made into words ending in *ing*, the *e* is lost.

bite	biting
come	coming
make	making
trouble	troubling
write	writing

Exceptions

singe	singeing (to keep the soft g)
agree	agreeing (to keep the ee sound)
flee	fleeing (to keep the ee sound)
hoe	hoeing
dye (colour)	dyeing

With some verbs *ie* is replaced by *y*

die	dying
lie	lying

6 If an adjective (see Table 34) ends in *l*, the corresponding adverb (which answers the question: How?) ends in *lly*.

adjective	*adverb*
beautiful	beautifully
faithful	faithfully
hopeful	hopefully
peaceful	peacefully
spiteful	spitefully

7 Some adjectives that end in *y* have corresponding adverbs and nouns in which the *y* is replaced by an *i*.

adjective	*adverb*	*noun*
busy	busily	business
merry	merrily	merriment

Many people have difficulty in spelling some words correctly because they are unable to distinguish, for example, between there and their, it's and its, book and book's, books and books'. If you cannot decide which to use, you need only remember how to indicate ownership. That is to say, you must learn how to indicate the possession of something.

Their and *theirs* are used to indicate that something belongs to a person or thing. *There* is used with a verb. Remember: there is, there are, there was, there were – t h e r e spells there. This spelling is also used for a place. Is anyone there? There is their house, over there.

My, his, her, *its*, our, your and *their* are possessive adjectives: my book, her eyes, its leaves, and their house. Mine, his, hers, *its*, ours, yours and *theirs* are possessive pronouns. This book is mine; this is yours; and these are *theirs*. Remember this rule: e in her, i in his, e and i in their.

It's means it is or it has, can't means cannot, don't means do not, that's means that is, they're means they are, who's means who is, and won't means will not. However, unless you are writing to a friend, or reporting a conversation in quotation marks, it is best to avoid such contractions (see colloquial English, p. 63).

An s is added to many nouns (names of things, see Table 34) to make them plural: book becomes books; but man becomes men. To indicate ownership either an apostrophe s ('s) is added to a word (book's and men's) or just an apostrophe is added (books'). For example: the cat's dinner (the dinner of the cat); the cats' dinner (the dinner of the cats); the man's books (the books of the man); the men's books (the books of the men); the books' covers (the covers of the books); the book's cover (the cover of the book).

Write Dr Smith's office (for the office of Dr Smith); but *either* Dr Jones' office *or* Dr Jones's office is acceptable (for the office of Dr Jones).

Note that 1990's music (apostrophe before the s) is the music of 1990, and 1990s' music (apostrophe after the s) is the music of the 1990s (the ten years 1990 to 1999), no apostrophe being required when simply forming the plural (see p. 177).

Do not add an apostrophe and s, to indicate ownership, to a word that in itself indicates ownership (a possessive adjective or a possessive pronoun – see list on pp. 182–3). The only exceptions are one, -one and -body, as in one's, someone's, everyone's, no-body's, somebody's and everybody's.

IMPROVE YOUR WRITING

1 *Exercises in dictation,* with first seen and then unseen passages, provide practice in both punctuation and spelling; and help you to increase your writing speed. You also learn about your subject if exercises in dictation are given by teachers of other subjects as well as by teachers of English.

When teachers dictate notes, they should check that important words are spelt correctly, either by marking the work or by writing these words on the blackboard at the end of the dictation so that the students can check their own work.

2 *Keep a good dictionary on your bookshelf* (see p. 186), available for reference when you are thinking, reading or writing. Make a note, from your dictionary, of the spelling of any word corrected by an assessor. It is a good idea to keep an indexed notebook for this purpose so that you can try not to spell any word incorrectly more than once. It is better to memorize the correct spelling of any word you find you have spelt incorrectly than to rely on a spell checker (see p. 169), and you will not be able to use a spell checker in examinations.

3 *Spelling test.* Ask someone to test your spelling of these words:
   absence, accelerate, accidentally, accommodate, achieved, acquaint, address, altogether, already, analogous, ancillary, apparent, attendance, audience, auxiliary,
   beauty, beginning, bureaucracy,
   calendar, census, cereal, competence, conscience, conscientious, consensus, commitment, committee,
   definite, desiccated, desperate, develop, disappear, disappoint,
   embarrass, emperor, eradicate, exaggerate, existence,
   fascinate, forty, fourth, fulfil, fulfilled,
   gauge, glamorize, grammar,
   harassment, harmful, hierarchy, humorous,
   idiosyncrasy, incidentally, independent, irradiate,
   liaison,
   misspell, millennium, minuscule,
   necessary, noticeably,
   occasion, occurred, omit, omitted,
   parallel, personnel, possess, precede, privilege, procedure, proceed, pronunciation, publicly, pursued,
   receive, recommend, relevant, rhythm,
   scissors, seize, separate, severely, siege, successful, supersede, syllable,
   unnecessarily, until,
   wholly,
   yield.

4 Take an interest in the study of the origins of words (etymology). This will help you to understand why some words are spelt in a particular way. For example, the word separate is derived from a Latin word *separare* (to separate or divide); so is another English word, pare, meaning to cut one's nails or to peel (potatoes, for example); but desperate is from the Latin *sperare* (to hope), and means without hope.

5 Do not get into the habit of using another word when you are not sure of the spelling of the most appropriate word. Instead, always refer to a dictionary so that you can use the word that best conveys your meaning.

Further reading

DICTIONARIES

A good dictionary gives the spelling, pronunciation, and meaning of each word, its use in current English (for example, n = noun, colloq = colloquial, sl = slang), its derivatives (words formed from it), and its derivation (origins). Make sure your dictionary gives all this information. Suitable dictionaries for students include *Chambers' Twentieth Century Dictionary* (Chambers, Edinburgh), *Collins English Dictionary* (Collins, London), *The Concise Oxford Dictionary* (Oxford University Press, Oxford), and *Webster's New Collegiate Dictionary* (Meriam, Mass.).

REFERENCE BOOKS

Barrass, R. (1978), *Scientists Must Write: A Guide to Better Writing for Scientists, Engineers and Students*, London and New York, Chapman & Hall.

Barrass, R. (1984), *Study! A Guide to Effective Study, Revision and Examination Techniques*, London and New York, Chapman & Hall.

Flesch. R. F. (1962), *The Art of Plain Talk*, London and New York, Collier-Macmillan.

Fowler, H. W. (1974), *Dictionary of Modern English Usage*, 2nd edn rev. Sir Ernest Gowers, London, Oxford University Press.

Gash, S. (1989), *Effective Literature Searching for Students*, Aldershot, Gower.

Gowers, E. (1986), *The Complete Plain Words*, 3rd edn rev. S. Greenbaum and J. Whitcut, London, HMSO.

Napley, D. (1975), *The Technique of Persuasion*, 2nd edn London, Sweet & Maxwell.

Partridge, E. (1965), *Usage and Abusage: A Guide to Good English*, 8th edn, London and New York, Hamish Hamilton and British Book Centre.

Perrin, P. G. (1965), *Writer's Guide and Index to English*, 4th edn rev. K. W. Dickens and W. R. Ebbitt, Fair Lawn, N. J., Scott, Foresman & Co.

Quiller-Couch, A. (1916) *On the Art of Writing*, Cambridge, Cambridge University Press.

Vallins, G. H. (1964), *Good English: How to Write It*, London and Washington, André Deutsch and Academic Press.

Index